Behind the Facemask

A Child's Abuse, A Man's Redemption

by

Anthony James Hodel

©2025 44 MEDIA

Cleveland, Ohio

2025

Behind the Facemask: A Child's Abuse, A Man's Redemption
©2025 Anthony James Hodel

All rights reserved.

No part of this book may be reproduced, distributed, or transmitted in any form or by any means, including photocopying, recording, or other electronic or mechanical methods, without the prior written permission of the publisher, except in the case of brief quotations embodied in critical reviews, articles, or scholarly works.

Published by 44 MEDIA
Cleveland, Ohio, USA

ISBN: 979-8-9934632-0-9
USCO 1-5016805711

Cover design by Hodel Holdings, LLC
Printed in the United States of America

This is a work of nonfiction.

For information, permissions, or media inquiries, contact:
44 MEDIA / Hodel Holdings, LLC
www.hodelholdings.com

Dedication

To those who hurt me—

Thank you. You unknowingly forged a strength in me I didn't know I had. Every scar became a layer of armor. Every lie, every punch, every betrayal… became fuel. You thought you were breaking me—but you were building a warrior.

To my angels—

To the woman I called Grandma, though no blood bound us. A Black woman on 73rd and Kinsman in Cleveland who the world might've seen as unrelated, but who saved my life. I was sent to her house as punishment—suspended over 20 times, told to stay inside because the streets weren't "safe" for a white boy. But I found more peace there than I ever did at home. She taught me that love has no color, that dignity is shown through kindness, and that judging others is a sign of weakness, not strength. Her quiet grace and unconditional care remain stitched into the best parts of me.

To my brother, my best friend, Chris—

You walked into my life when I was lost, forced to leave Cleveland Heights, stripped of a future I was ready to conquer. I landed in Brunswick, a place that felt foreign and cold, where racism and resentment greeted me before any welcome did. But you saw me. You knew I was different—and you never flinched. You stood by me through fights, setbacks, and all the wildness of youth. You told me the truth when I didn't want to hear it, and you loved me anyway. I never needed a yes man—I needed a real one. And you, my brother, have always been that. I admire you deeply. You are the man I aspired to be—honorable, loyal, and unshakably good.

To my wife, Trisha—

You've seen the worst a man can show in a marriage, yet you stood by me when you had every reason not to. You waited for me to face the darkness I had buried for decades. You gave me space to confront my demons, grace when I didn't deserve it, and love that endured storms most would run from. I banked on you to fix what only I could heal—and you never gave up on me. Your strength and patience are beyond anything I've ever known. I love you endlessly, and I'm still working every day to become the man you deserve.

To my football coaches—

You were more than coaches. You were father figures when my own father chose the bottle over me. You taught me discipline, grit, and how to keep showing up—on the field and in life. You showed me that the team is bigger than the individual, that ego has no place in the locker room or in leadership. That mindset shaped how I approach business, relationships, and growth. You taught me to seek knowledge, to value other perspectives, and to look at life through someone else's lens. You gave me structure when I was lost—and those lessons echo in everything I do.

To Dr. Mike Dwyer—

God rest your soul. You weren't just a psychology professor. You were a mirror, a mentor, and a voice of brutal honesty when I needed it most. Our private conversations were my first breaths of truth—the beginning of learning how to speak what I had buried for decades. You shared your own life, your own failures, and you never once judged me. You always answered the phone, especially when I was in crisis. You were my go-to when I didn't trust anyone else to help me make sense of the chaos. Your wisdom still guides me. Your legacy lives in these pages.

This book is for those who saw me through the fog, held the line when I was slipping, and never let me forget that redemption is possible—even when the world tries to convince you otherwise.

Anthony James Hodel

Contents

Dedication	iii
Foreword	ix
Preface	xiii
Introduction	xv
Chapter 1: House of Hell	1
Chapter 2: When Child Services Failed Me	13
Chapter 3: A Ride That Saved My Life	33
Chapter 4: Friday Nights & Father Figures	41
Chapter 5: Muscle, Mayhem & Mexico	57
Chapter 6: The Circus Life	67
Chapter 7: The Silence of Shame	77
Chapter 8: The Mirror Doesn't Lie	91
Chapter 9: Facing Ghosts	105
Chapter 10: The Power of Entrepreneurship	129
Chapter 11: Fathers & Final Goodbyes	151
Chapter 12: BMW on Bando Lane	165
Chapter 13: Anger	175
Chapter 14: The 44 Foundation	185
Chapter 15: The Distance That Raised Me	193
Chapter 16: The Redemption Stairway	209
Chapter 17: Behind the Facemask	217
Chapter 18: Soul Under NDA	233
Full Circle	241
Final Words	271
Afterword	273
About the Author	275
Index	277

Anthony James Hodel

Foreword

I met Anthony about fifteen years ago under circumstances that seemed ordinary at the time but would prove to be the beginning of an extraordinary friendship. He had moved to Kansas to run a dealership where I was working as a Finance Manager. From our first conversation, there was an instant connection, a mutual respect and understanding for how we approached the business. Anthony, as with all of his businesses, was on the cutting edge of technology, using SEO and SMO as if he was a Chief Marketing Officer and not the GM of a dealership. We shared the language of hustle and grit that needed no translation. In Anthony, I had found a kindred spirit in our desire to be the best; to win and oh, we really loved sports and women!

We'd close out the day and head to a local cigar lounge, where the conversations would stretch into the night. We talked about deals, about life, about relationships, about what it means to build something from nothing. I remember when Anthony, first told me about the warranty company he owned, and while I was familiar with it, I did not know he was the owner. It was hard to imagine that a guy who once had an 8-figure net worth was now sitting in a cigar lounge in Wichita, KS, as an employee of anybody. Anthony, had this intensity about him, a drive that was impossible to ignore and equally impossible to fully understand. I knew he had been wildly successful, and I knew that somehow, he would be successful again, it was a matter of when not if. I knew he was relentless. What I didn't know, what I couldn't have known, was the weight he carried every single day.

Reading *Behind the Facemask* opened my eyes to so much I never knew about the man I called my friend. The stories we shared while smoking cigars were real, but they were only the surface. Beneath the confidence, the business acumen, the insatiable lust for women and sex and let's not forget about the wins, I now realize was a man fighting battles most of us will never face. Battles that began long before he ever shook my hand or sat across from me at that lounge.

This book is not what I would call an easy read. It's not for the faint of heart, or prudish, and at times, it's deeply uncomfortable. But it's also necessary. Anthony doesn't ask for your sympathy, nor do I think he ever would. What he offers instead is his truth, laid bare in a way that most of us, especially men will never have the courage to do. He pulls back the mask we all wear and shows you what's underneath: the pain, the rage, the shame, the guilt, and ultimately, the fight for redemption.

What struck me most about this book is not just what Anthony went through, but how he refused to let survival be the end of his story. I told Anthony, if I had an ex-wife trying to take any semblance of happiness, I made for myself, and lost all of that money, I don't know how'd I recover. Anthony didn't just endure his trauma, he interrogated it, wrestled with it, and eventually transformed it into purpose. The man who once buried his pain under muscle, money, women, sex and endless motion is now using that same energy to break the silence that traps so many men in their own private hells.

For every man reading this who has ever felt like he couldn't speak, like his pain didn't matter, like strength meant silence, this book is for you. Anthony isn't just telling his story. He's giving you a blueprint for overcoming your own demons.

In the pages that follow, you'll meet a man I thought I knew. You'll also meet the boy he once was, the battles he's fought, and the lessons he's learned the hard way. You'll see that redemption isn't a destination, it's daily practice, it's a decision to be better every day. And you'll understand that the real measure of a man isn't whether he falls, but whether he gets back up, does the work, and helps others do the same.

Anthony, my friend, thank you for your courage. Thank you for refusing to let shame win. And thank you for showing the rest of us that it's never too late to take off the mask and start living in the truth.

This is more than a book. It's a roadmap for men who are ready to climb out of their own darkness. And it all begins with turning the page.

> **—Dr. Tyrone Cassell (A Friend Who Didn't Know the Full Story, Until Now)**

Anthony James Hodel

Preface

Some books are written to entertain. Others to educate. This one was written to survive.

From the outside, my life might look like the American dream — business success, accolades, and a relentless drive that could bulldoze through any obstacle. But behind that façade was a boy who learned to hide his pain behind a football helmet, a polished smile, and a work ethic that wasn't born from ambition, but from desperation.

This isn't a story of victimhood. It's a story of war. A war fought in hallways where slammed doors became battle drums, in bedrooms where the darkness held more danger than comfort, and in a world that looked away when the bruises were too obvious to ignore.

Football saved me. It gave me structure when chaos was the norm, brotherhood when blood failed me, and a map to manhood when I was lost in the fog of abuse, addiction, and rage. But sports alone weren't the cure — the real battle was inside. Facing what happened to me. Forgiving the unforgivable. Learning that strength isn't just lifting weight in a gym — it's lifting the weight off your soul.

This book will take you through the house of horrors that shaped me, the systems that failed me, the addictions that nearly consumed me, and the moments of grace that pulled me back from the edge. You'll see the man I became — not in spite of my past, but because I refused to let it define my future.

If you've ever carried scars no one can see… if you've been silenced, overlooked, or broken… if you're still searching for a way to take your power back — this is for you.

It's not an easy read. It's not meant to be. But I promise you this: by the last page, you'll believe that even in the darkest places, redemption is possible.

— Anthony James Hodel

Introduction

When people look at me today, they see the entrepreneur, the leader, the man who built companies and created opportunities where there were none. What they don't see is the boy who grew up inside a prison he never deserved, where abuse and silence became my daily reality.

This book is my unmasking. Each chapter pulls back another layer of the life I've carried — the good, the bad, the ugly, and the redemption I had to fight for.

It begins with "House of Hell," where I take you back into the footsteps and slammed doors that haunted my childhood home. Then comes "When Child Services Failed Me," a story of a broken system that looked away when I needed it most.

But this isn't just about suffering — it's about the escapes, the lifelines, the people and moments that gave me hope. "A Ride That Saved My Life" shares how one unexpected drive set me on a path I might not have survived without. In "Friday Nights & Father Figures," you'll see how football and the men around it gave me discipline, brotherhood, and a glimpse of manhood that wasn't soaked in violence.

The road wasn't straight. "Muscle, Mayhem & Mexico" dives into the chaos of my young adulthood — strength and violence intertwined, adrenaline masking pain. "Anger" shows how the rage I never faced in childhood grew into a monster I carried into relationships, walls, windshields, and everything in my path.

But there's redemption too. In "His Final Days, My First Peace," you'll walk with me through the hardest goodbye of my life — watching my father suffer and pass, and the perspective that loss gave me. In "The Power of Entrepreneurship," you'll see how building businesses wasn't just about money — it was my therapy, my proving ground, and my way to rewrite the story I was given.

The book closes with "The Redemption Stairway," where I reflect on the climb out of silence, and "The Silence of Shame," where I finally speak the words I buried for decades.

This is not a comfortable read. It's not meant to be. But it is honest. It's a journey through abuse, addiction, rage, and survival — and into faith, forgiveness, and redemption.

If you've ever felt like your past is a weight you can't escape, I hope these pages show you something different: that the past is not a prison — it can be a platform. That even the ugliest scars can become someone else's map.

I broke my silence to write this.
Maybe in these pages, you'll find the courage to break yours too.

— Anthony James Hodel

Chapter 1:

House of Hell

"Home wasn't safe. It was a battlefield."

The Footsteps in the Hall

Night taught me vigilance. I learned the rhythm of shoes on the hallway floor and the way a door handle pauses just before it turns. Lying still, I measured distance and time with my breath, bracing for what the next minute might bring. In that house, safety was an illusion; the quiet only meant the trouble hadn't arrived yet.

Nothing ever happened in public—at least nothing I can remember. It was always inside those walls. No matter how loud it felt, the screams didn't travel; the house swallowed sound. We lived in an average home on a respectable, diverse block. People waved, mowed lawns, went to work. Everyone seemed busy in their own world—not noticing, and, truthfully, neither did the authorities. Harm can hide behind a front door that looks perfectly normal.

Life Inside Four Walls

Daylight didn't reset anything. My father drank and lashed out. My mother cycled through untreated highs and lows that could change the temperature of the home in an instant—most mornings began with raised voices and slammed cabinet doors. To this day, if a morning starts loud, I feel my body fold in. In jail, reveille and the shouting at count time were the hardest part; it sounded like home in the worst way.

My older brother filled the space between with cruelty and violations of trust. I didn't have words for it then. Part of me bargained, he's my brother; he wouldn't make me do something wrong, right? That confusion is what happens when harm is wrapped in secrecy and mixed signals. With what I know now, none of it was my fault. The silence I kept wasn't weakness; it was survival. In late childhood, the boundary violations were recurring, and once the harm escalated from frequent oral sex to penetration. That moment fractured how I understood closeness and safety for years, even today.

I've been told that as an infant I was injured—lifted by one arm, leaving a broken arm and a dislocated shoulder. Even my earliest chapter carried harm, whether I remembered it or not.

I also remember the belt—anger riding its length in a string of strikes. "Stop crying or there will be more," I was told, and I learned to go silent mid-sob. Some nights the punishment was hunger; "go to bed" meant no dinner. Sleep became my safest bet.

There are two memories of my father that I will never forget—etched so deeply into my mind that even time can't dull their edges. The first was when I was around eight or ten years old. He came home so drunk one night that he stumbled into my bedroom in a fog of confusion, thinking my bed was the bathroom. Before I could even process what was happening, he urinated all over me and the sheets. I remember freezing—too stunned, too young to understand. My mother cleaned the mattress and, in fear that it might happen again, covered it with plastic. Days later, my friends saw it and teased me, thinking I was a bed wetter. The humiliation burned, but the truth was even worse. I swallowed it, buried it, and let them believe their version. That shame stuck with me; even now, I can still feel that same sting like it happened yesterday.

The second memory came years later, in my teens. My father had a flat tire, the bolts rusted tight, and nothing—WD-40, Coke, even heat—would loosen them. I offered to help, using my strength to push down on the breaker bar, but it wouldn't budge. He was drunk again, his words slurred and sharp. "Move the fuck out of the way," he barked. I told him, "Hold on, I almost got it." Before I could finish, pain exploded through my back as he struck me with the bar. I hit the ground, dazed and humiliated, but something inside me snapped. I stood up, looked him dead in the eyes, and told him never to touch me again. Then I swung—one clean shot to the jaw. It broke. He never laid a hand on me after that. I've carried guilt over that moment ever since, especially after his death. But I also know it was a defining moment—a line drawn in blood and pain. Sometimes, protecting your mental and physical health means standing up, even when it hurts like hell.

Even as a kid, I knew something was off with my mom. The highs and lows weren't moodiness; they were illness. Only after she died did I learn the fuller truth: she, too, had been abused at every level, and as an infant in the 1940s, she was abandoned and taken in by a Black woman—what people in that era would have called a "colored woman." Society wasn't ready for that story, and the pressure and stigma around race bent a life before it had a chance to grow straight. I never got to sit with my mother and hear it from her. I caught fragments—half sentences, abrupt subject changes—because she lived in survival mode and never had the safety to face it, let alone speak it. Counseling taught me to read those silences. Knowing her history didn't excuse what I lived through, but it explained the weather in our house and helped me stop taking on blame that was never mine.

The Silence Between Hits

We didn't talk about any of it. That was the first rule. Don't name it, don't show it, and if someone asks, say we're fine. I mistook that silence for strength and carried it into adulthood. I never harmed a child and never wanted to—but pain finds exits. Mine came out as drinking, infidelity, and choosing chaos because peace felt like a setup.

I didn't say the truest sentence until I was thirty-two, and even then I said it like it belonged to someone else. Looking back, I see why I hid it: in a dangerous house, the brain prioritizes survival over storytelling. You don't process—you partition.

What still puzzles me is this: I don't remember my brother getting beaten. He wasn't a good student—bad grades, drugs, the whole slide—and yet I don't recall the same punishments landing on him. I was acting out too, but I also knew I was gifted. Balancing those two truths—troublemaker and talented—was a private tug-of-war. In a house that rewarded silence and punished honesty, being "smart" felt like another secret to hide, another edge to sand down. That confusion didn't excuse anyone; it just shows how pain distributes itself unevenly in a family and how a kid can learn to perform one self while protecting another.

The Mask I Wore Outside

Outside the front door, I learned how to perform. I smiled at school, cracked jokes, hit my marks, and kept my story clean for neighbors and relatives. I tried to be useful so people wouldn't ask questions. That habit of performance became a second skin. When you grow up waiting for footsteps, calm makes you suspicious. I built walls high enough to keep danger out—and just as effectively kept love out too.

People always complimented my bright blue eyes. Funny thing: the same eyes that drew attention also told on me. In certain phases of my life, I can see the pain sitting there, clear as a summer sky. When I look back at old photos now, I can timestamp the hurt—that half-smile, that faraway stare— "yep, this is when I was going through it." Those "pretty blues" were a mask for everyone else and a mirror for me.

The Quiet I Found Outside

I did have good memories, and I built them myself. I shoveled snow at dawn, raked leaves until my hands blistered, and cut lawns all over the neighborhood—any job I could take. Not because I loved money, but because it got me out of the house. Work meant I was safe and alone. If I wasn't working, I walked the streets or went to the lake and let the water do the talking. Those hours outside were proof that peace existed somewhere—and that I could earn it.

Sometimes my parents would shake their heads and say, "You made more than us today," and I didn't understand how that could be. I was nine or ten. My entire business model was simple: go do it. Knock on doors and ask—Want your grass cut? Driveway shoveled? Leaves raked? Almost nobody said no to a kid who took the initiative. That's when I learned a quiet truth: if you ask, you create a margin of error big enough for opportunity to walk through. This simple idea applies to everything—life, sports, business, dating.

I cared about the work, too. Edges straight, walks swept, porches cleared. Without knowing the terms, I was already upselling. "I can trim the hedges while I'm here," and asking for referrals. "Do you think your neighbor might want theirs done?" Looking back, it's wild to realize how much I understood: show up, do it well, ask for more. Outside, with a rake or a shovel in my hands, I wasn't the kid waiting for footsteps. I was the kid building something of his own.

A House I Shouldn't Have Been In

There was another place my parents left me when my mother worked—a grungy house with nicotine walls and old coffee air. The adult in charge there was volatile and unsafe. Once he hurt me and burned my arm with a lighter. When my dad picked me up, I showed him the injury. He went back inside and delivered a warning I can still hear: "Touch my kid again and I'll kill you." We never went back. As an adult, I can't shake the sense that harm was happening in that house long before I ever got there.

There was also a teenage "babysitter" whose behavior toward me was repeatedly inappropriate. I never said anything then—she was older, and part of me liked the attention. Looking back as a father, if one of my own kids went through that at ten, I would lose it. Two things can be true at once—a child can feel flattered and still be harmed. Naming it that way gives the kid I was the protection he didn't have.

There was a heaviness in that house that went beyond the nicotine-stained walls and stale coffee air. The man in charge was not just volatile—he was dangerous. His behavior made the space feel like a trap, and the teenage girl who was supposed to be a babysitter blurred every boundary. She was sixteen, I was ten, and what happened between us wasn't normal, wasn't safe, and wasn't okay. At the time, I didn't have the language to name it. I felt confused, scared, and strangely complicit because part of me didn't know how to reject the attention. But looking back now, I see it clearly: it was abuse. That house was a place where harm lived openly. The man would walk around half-dressed, exposing himself without shame. I suspect now that his own daughter was a victim too. What happened to me wasn't isolated—it was part of a larger sickness in that home. Naming it doesn't erase the past, but it gives the boy I was a voice he didn't have then. And that matters.

Reflection & Gut Punch

I wasn't living. I was surviving—and you can survive for years without ever learning to live.

My turning point didn't look like a movie. It was a prison camp—sixteen months for unpaid child support—where there was nowhere to hide from myself. That's where the nightmares returned, sharp enough that I could feel the staircase under my palms and smell the hallway air. The memories clarified what I had spent decades blurring: the harm was real, and it rewired me. I couldn't outwork or outdrink it. I had to face it.

Later in life, I finally asked my brother a question I needed more than an answer: Who did this to you? What made you like this? I wasn't hunting for an apology; I wanted the origin—who taught you this, when did it start, how did it get into our house? He offered fragments and deflection. No clean answer. What I took instead was a truth: trauma doesn't invent itself; it gets handed down until someone refuses to pass it along.

Forgiveness, for me, wasn't a pardon. It was a wire cutter. It didn't excuse anything; it cut the line tying my life to other people's hands. After that came the real work—steady, unglamorous, daily: telling the truth when lying would be easier, putting down the bottle, not sending the text, breathing when my chest told me to swing, and catching myself before I turned love into a battlefield again. Some days I won. Some days I failed hard. Then I got up and tried again. That's what healing looks like.

What Trauma Does to a Growing Body and Brain

From a medical and psychological point of view, childhood trauma isn't just a "bad memory." It's biology, psychology, and development colliding. A child's brain and body are still wiring themselves; repeated danger pushes that wiring toward survival over learning, connection, and play.

Stress System on Overdrive. The body's alarm network—the amygdala and stress hormones like cortisol and adrenaline—stays primed. In kids, that can hardwire hyper-vigilance: jumpiness, scanning rooms, trouble relaxing or sleeping. Over time this "always-on" state contributes to headaches, stomach issues, chronic pain, blood pressure changes, and fatigue.

Memory and Meaning. Traumatic stress can fragment memory. Some details go vivid, others go blank. The brain prioritizes "keep me safe" over "make a neat story," so later reminders (sounds, smells, seasons) can trigger alarms even when there's no present danger.

Attention and Learning. When the nervous system is guarding the exits, focusing in class or planning for the future is harder. That isn't laziness—it's biology rerouting energy into protection.

Attachment and Trust. If harm comes from inside the home, the map for closeness gets distorted. People can feel dangerous and isolation can feel safer. In adulthood this can look like cling-tight attachment, avoidance, or swinging between both.

Coping That Looks Like "Bad Behavior." Numbing with substances, food, or work; dissociation; perfectionism; rage; shutting down—often creative survival strategies that outlive the danger.

Allostatic Load (Body Wear-and-Tear). Carrying stress for years taxes immune, cardiovascular, and metabolic systems. Early adverse experiences correlate with higher risks for later health problems—the more early adversity, the higher the risk.

The Good News: Brains Can Heal. With safety, consistent support, and evidence-based care (trauma-informed CBT, EMDR, group work), the nervous system can learn new patterns. Triggers soften. Sleep returns. Relationships feel less like minefields. Healing isn't instant—but it's real.

Plainly put: when trauma happens to a child, the scars often travel into adulthood—physically and psychologically. But scars are also proof of healing. With the right help, the same brain that learned to survive can learn to live.

Self-Help Action Plan — Own It, Don't Let It Own You

Ownership Reframe (Daily)

Three truths:

- I didn't choose what happened.
- It does not own me.
- I own my story—and what happens next.

One-line pledge: It happened. It isn't me. I decide the next move.

Confront It (Safely, Not Suddenly)

Tell one person: a trusted friend, mentor, or licensed therapist.

Simple script: "Something happened to me when I was a kid. I'm working on it now. I don't need fixing—I need a witness and support."

If contact with anyone who harmed you exists: write boundaries (time, topics, access) and review them with your witness/therapist.

Build a Safety Net

Save three numbers: one friend, one professional, one crisis line.

For 30 days, limit triggers (people, places, substances, media) while you stabilize.

Body first: sleep 7–8 hrs; move 20–30 min/day; use 4×4 breathing (inhale 4, hold 4, exhale 4, hold 4) when triggered.

Talk It Through (Therapy & Tools)

Options: trauma-informed CBT, EMDR, or a survivor group.

Five-minute journal prompts:

- What did I feel today? Where in my body?
- What boundary did I hold (or need)?
- One sentence of truth I'm willing to say out loud.

Invest for ROI in Your Personal Stock

- Define your assets: Health, Relationships, Skills, Purpose, Finances.
- Daily 60–90-minute Investment Block: pick one asset and do one high-return action.
- Track returns weekly: energy (0–10), mood (0–10), relationships (better/same/worse), money (+/–). Double down on what moves the needle.

30-Day Sprint (Repeatable)

- Week 1: Tell your witness/therapist. Establish sleep, movement, and the daily pledge.

- Week 2: Add one boundary. Do the Investment Block 4 days.
- Week 3: Share one harder truth in therapy. Replace one numbing habit with a skill habit.
- Week 4: Review your Personal P&L: gains (where did I feel free/clear?), costs (what drains me?), next bets (two assets to invest in next month).

Trigger & Relapse Plan

When triggered: name it → breathe 4×4 for 90 sec → text/call your witness → move your body 10 min → write three lines about the trigger (facts/feelings; no analysis).

If you slip (drink, lash out, isolate): log it without shame, make amends if needed, and restart the next block. Data, not drama.

Green Flags

You tell the truth sooner. Fewer blowups; faster recovery.

Boundaries feel less scary. The past shows up less—and leaves faster.

Bottom line: You didn't choose the events. They don't own you. Own the story, invest daily, and compound the returns.

Anthony James Hodel

Chapter 2:
When Child Services Failed Me

"The bruises healed. The silence didn't."

The Knock at the Door

Three sharp raps. My stomach dropped like the floor had vanished beneath me.

That knock always meant the same thing: caseworkers—clipboards, polite smiles, the smell of burnt coffee and bureaucracy. My mother's eyes would slice through me with a look that said, *say nothing. Smile. Don't you dare ruin this.*

So, I smiled with a split lip and rehearsed lies in my throat. "We were horse-playing." "Just wrestling." "It was an accident." They wrote it down, nodded, said all the right words, and left. The moment their taillights disappeared, the real punishment began.

At school it was the same performance—forms, signatures, phrases like "welfare check." Nobody ever asked the question I needed:

What really happens when you go home?

What happens, statistically, is that most cases never even become cases. In FY 2023, U.S. child-protection hotlines received an estimated **4.4 million referrals**, about **7.78 million** children. **More than half (52.5%) were screened out at the front door**—no investigation. Among the children who *did* get a CPS response (**~3.08 million**), only **546,159** were officially determined to be "victims" (**~17.7%**). The rest were closed as "non-victim" or otherwise concluded, even though **about 71% of reports come from professionals** like teachers, doctors, and police. States also report that **only ~20% of non-victims** receive post-response services; **56% of victims** do.

One caseworker—thin glasses, kind voice—actually crouched to my level once. "Anthony, how are things at home?"

My shoulder throbbed from the morning's belt. My hands shook in my lap. For a second, I almost told her. But my mother's warning glare filled my head.

"Just roughhousing," I said.

"Boys will be boys." She smiled, wrote it down, and closed her folder—closing my case with it.

They never saw me. They logged visits, drove away, and left me to face the aftermath.

Federal research helps explain why. In the National Incidence Study (the government's sentinel study that tracks maltreatment recognized by community professionals), **the majority of maltreated children recognized by professionals were *not* investigated by CPS**. In the most recent cycle, only **~32%** (strict "Harm" standard) to **~43%** (broader "Endangerment" standard) received an investigation—and **for school-recognized cases it was 20% or less**. The same study concluded that **if those children had been reported according to agency screening policies, CPS would have investigated most of them**; the authors infer that **mandated reporters fail to report "two-thirds or more" of those uninvestigated children**.

What they didn't see—what they couldn't see—was that my mother had been threatening to "get rid of me" for years. She'd spit venom like, "I should've had an abortion," or "I'll give you away and be done with you." Words that cut deeper than the belt ever could.

When the chance finally came for Child Services to take me—when she could've had me ruled "unruly" or surrendered me to the state—both my parents folded like a lawn chair. They didn't want the scandal; they wanted the problem to stay behind closed doors. Looking back, I understand their choice wasn't love. It was fear—fear of public perception, fear of legal trouble. They kept me because they were scared of what people would say, not because they chose me.

That silence has a pattern. In substantiated cases of child sexual abuse, **about one in four children later recant**—not because the abuse didn't happen, but often because of **pressure, fear, and lack of caregiver support**. Research finds recantation is most common when the abuser is a parent figure and the nonoffending caregiver is unsupportive.

If you're counting on the knock at the door to save a child, know this: **by age 18, more than a third of U.S. children will have been the subject of a CPS investigation**, but **only about one in eight will ever have maltreatment confirmed**. The funnel is wide at the top and narrow at the bottom—and it misses many kids completely.

The Dog That Found Me

I ran away so often it became a ritual—always in the fall, when the wind stung and the nights were too long. Smart timing, right?

No matter how far I went, my dog always found me. Loyal. Stubborn. My shadow. I'd crouch behind a neighbor's house, certain this time I'd vanish. Then I'd hear it—his nails on the sidewalk, the panting. He'd sit beside me like a furry detective, waiting. When I didn't move, he'd trot home and rat me out.

He didn't mean betrayal; he meant love. That kind of loyalty carved a place in me that never closed. It's why dogs still undo me—they love without asking, without judging, without leaving. Back then, he was the only one who made me feel safe.

It's no wonder I've carried a divine love for animals my entire life. They saved me when people wouldn't. To this day I donate to the ASPCA and want to rescue any that crosses my path. If I ever had billion-dollar money, I'd buy land until I couldn't buy more and build a sanctuary for every species that needed shelter—wild and domestic. I love my dogs more than my own life sometimes. They offer pure, unfiltered love.

I used to go mess with them in their personal space—pushing my brother or my dad until they pushed back—just to get my dog to attack. He literally would bite their arm if I yelled or was touched by them. I did it because feeling numb felt worse than pain; I wanted a reaction, anything to prove I still existed. Looking back, that's ugly and shameful, and the memory sits in me like glass. The dog's loyalty was sacred, even when I used it for something dark, and that contradiction taught me more about love than any sermon could.

The Dog That Found Me captures something researchers keep finding in the lab: contact with a calm, trusted animal can quiet a stormed nervous system. Short, gentle interactions—petting, stroking, even shared eye contact—are linked to lower levels of cortisol (the body's primary stress hormone) and to rises in oxytocin, a neurochemical tied to bonding, safety, and trust. Those biological shifts help explain the felt experience you describe: steadier breathing, a little more room to think, and the sense that you're not alone. Reviews of human–dog interaction show these effects across ages and settings, from classrooms to clinics.

Why dogs?

Lots of species can soothe us, but dogs bring an unusually helpful mix of traits for trauma and mood care. Through millennia of coevolution, they've become exquisitely attuned to people—able to read our pointing and gaze, and to respond to human facial emotion and tone—so they notice and orient to early signs of distress. They also accept (and often seek) touch, which matters because slow, rhythmic contact is one of the most reliable ways to downshift arousal. Add trainability and a desire to work with humans, and you get an animal that can provide steady, nonjudgmental presence **and learn tasks that interrupt spirals: deep-pressure therapy, "create space" behaviors in crowds, room checks before sleep, or waking someone from a nightmare. Research on dog–human bonding and emotion perception helps account for these advantages.

For people recovering from abuse and complex trauma, dogs can be both lifelines and—too often—a barrier to safety. A synthesis of 12 studies found that **18–48%** of domestic-violence survivors delayed leaving or returned to an abuser out of concern for their pets; other work reports that **48–71%** of pet-owning survivors say their partner also threatened or harmed the animal. Making shelters pet-friendly (or creating foster "safe havens") removes a painful tradeoff and preserves a vital source of emotional regulation during crisis.

Clinical impact when dogs are integrated into care.

- In the largest U.S. clinical trial to date of psychiatric service dogs for military-related PTSD (**n = 156**), adding a trained service dog to usual care was associated with **lower PTSD**

symptom severity, anxiety, and depression after 3 months, based on both self-report and blinded clinician ratings. These partnerships also improved aspects of daily functioning.

- In emergency medicine, a randomized trial in 2025 showed that a **10-minute therapy-dog visit** produced a **significantly greater drop in children's anxiety** (compared with standard child-life support alone) within 45 minutes; parents' ratings fell, too. Effects were modest but clinically useful in a setting where fear is high and medications are common.

- Early physiological work in veterans with PTSD also points to improvements in sleep and activity patterns after service-dog pairing, consistent with stabilization of daily rhythms that support recovery.

"They save our lives" isn't just a feeling—there are numbers.

- A meta-analysis of 10 studies (3.8 million people) in *Circulation* found that dog ownership is associated with a **24% lower risk of all-cause mortality** and a **31% lower risk of cardiovascular death**. Among people who'd already had a coronary event, living with a dog was linked to a **65% lower risk of death** during follow-up. These are associations, not proof of causation, but they suggest a powerful protective pattern, likely through more movement, routine, and social connection.

- Part of that protection is simply getting us moving: in one population study, dog owners walked their dogs a median **220 minutes per week**—activity that is strongly tied to mood and heart health.

- Some trained dogs alert to dangerous health changes. For people with insulin-treated diabetes, several studies report that "diabetes alert dogs" detect a high proportion of hypoglycemic episodes—one program reported **median sensitivity ~83%**—though other studies find **high false-alarm rates** and emphasize that dogs **don't replace** medical devices like continuous glucose monitors. Even with limits, timely alerts can help avert injury.

Putting the bond to work—safely.
My reflection on having once "weaponized" a dog's loyalty is important. The same devotion that steadies us can be misused in conflict. Today's best practice is to protect the animal–human bond with clear boundaries: choose stable, people-oriented dogs; prioritize force-free training; give the dog regular decompression (walks, play, sleep); and, if trauma is part of the picture, involve a clinician and a reputable service/therapy-dog organization so tasks are taught to help (interrupt panic, anchor at night, lead to an exit) rather than to escalate confrontations. That keeps the loyalty sacred—and turns it into a predictable, healthy form of care.

Quick stats at a glance

- Pet–dog contact can **lower cortisol** and **raise oxytocin**, which helps calm stress and supports bonding.

- **PTSD service dogs**: lower PTSD severity, anxiety, and depression vs. usual care at 3 months.

- **Therapy dogs in the ER**: children's anxiety fell more with a 10-minute visit than with standard support alone.

- **Longevity**: dog ownership linked with **24% lower all-cause** and **31% lower cardiovascular** mortality; **65% lower** all-cause mortality after a prior coronary event.

- **Domestic violence**: **18–48%** of survivors delay leaving/return due to pet safety; **48–71%** report pet threats or harm.

Bad Boy School & The Last Fight

To my best recollection, trouble at school ramped up fast. I was getting in fights, making daily trips to the principal's office, serving suspensions. Eventually they expelled me and sent me to what they called "bad boy school."

I attended Northwood—an institutional place covered in green tile that felt like a prison. If you talked out of turn, teachers could physically grab you and restrain you on the ground. That was their "correction." It was a place designed to break you if you let it.

But before Northwood, there was the final fight that changed everything. It started like so many others—a shove in the hallway, a stupid comment, the usual build-up of humiliation. I snapped. We went outside near the cracked concrete by the bike racks, and I grabbed him. The move came out of me the way survival instincts do: a pile-driver, WWF-style. Concrete met neck with a sound that should never be a child's memory.

He went limp. When he woke up, he had a concussion and a neck injury. Teachers panicked. Parents yelled. Ambulances came. I was suspended, and the paperwork labeled me "dangerous." They expelled me shortly after. That fight was the last straw—my anger had turned real and irreversible.

At Northwood I lost even more school time. I was only allowed to return when the social workers and the shrinks said I could. I went crazy in those rooms—screaming, crying, pleading to leave. Only after the professionals cleared me was I permitted to go back to the school everyone already knew where I'd been. I was held back that year for missing so much school; I failed epically.

Today I tell parents bluntly: if your kid's grades tank, don't just assume laziness. Investigate what's happening at home or in their personal life. Academic failure and personal trauma walk hand in hand. You might be seeing the symptom and missing the cause.

For years I replayed that fight and asked myself if I'd meant to kill him. At the time, it didn't shock me I felt that way. I was that tired. Later, when guilt hit, it landed like a cold hand on my chest. Damage breeds damage.

Do "Tough" Schools Heal—or Harden—Kids Like Me?

People ask me whether a military-style school could have helped—a place with uniforms, drill, and harsh consequences to "straighten me out." If you've lived through abuse, your body is already wired for threat. What looks like structure to an outsider can feel like danger to a kid whose nervous system never got to stand down. More force didn't teach me control; it taught me to scan for exits.

There's a difference between **structure** and **severity**. Structure is predictable, consistent, and anchored in relationships. Severity is control for control's sake—public shaming, zero tolerance, and hands on kids to make a point. The first can steady a traumatized child. The second usually backfires. Even pediatric and education authorities now say flat out: corporal punishment and "get-tough" discipline don't improve behavior and often cause harm; physical restraint is not a correction tool and should never be used as punishment. It is an emergency safety measure only, and only to prevent imminent serious harm.

If you want evidence of how wrong we sometimes get this, look at the numbers. Students with disabilities are a small slice of enrollment but make up a large share of those secluded or mechanically restrained in U.S. schools—disparities that mirror how punishment gets misapplied when behavior is actually communication of distress. That's not "accountability"; that's a system missing the signal

Here's the hard truth I learned the long way: **you can't punish trauma out of a child.** Abuse and other adverse childhood experiences change stress systems and attention, memory, and learning. When school becomes a battlefield, the brain goes to war and class is lost. Healing starts with safety, predictability, and adults who co-regulate before they "correct." Trauma-informed approaches exist for exactly this reason.

What about "boot camps," "last-chance academies," or the wider "troubled teen" industry? Oversight agencies have documented thousands of abuse allegations—including deaths—over the years. And rigorous reviews show that the classic scared-straight/boot-camp model doesn't deter; if anything, it can make outcomes worse. When programs show benefits, it's because they deliver real therapy, education, and mentoring—not because someone yelled louder or used tighter control.

There is nuance. Some **voluntary, education-first** programs that feel "military-flavored" but are not punitive—for example, the National Guard Youth ChalleNGe model—have credible evidence for improving graduation and GED attainment among older teens. But that's about schooling and mentorship; it is **not** a treatment for trauma, and it doesn't justify using restraint or humiliation as discipline.

So what actually helps a kid like me?

- **A safe, predictable school climate** that uses de-escalation, not humiliation. School-wide Positive Behavioral

Interventions and Supports (PBIS) reduce exclusionary discipline and are associated with less use of seclusion/restraint.

- **Trauma-informed programming** in school (mindfulness/skills groups, regulated classrooms, trained staff) to stabilize attention, mood, and relationships.

- **Evidence-based family and individual treatments**—Trauma-Focused CBT, Parent-Child Interaction Therapy, and Multisystemic Therapy—delivered by licensed clinicians. These reduce trauma symptoms and disruptive behavior and can lower out-of-home placements.

If you're evaluating a "strict" or "military-style" option, here are **non-negotiables**:

1. **No corporal punishment, no seclusion rooms, and no planned use of restraint as discipline.** Restraint only in emergencies to prevent imminent serious harm; incidents are documented, debriefed, and reported to families.

2. **Licensed mental-health staff on site** using named, evidence-based therapies (TF-CBT, PCIT, MST). If what they offer is "life coaching," "tough love," or "behavior modification" without specifics, that's a red flag.

3. **School-wide PBIS or equivalent**, with regular data reviews on suspensions, restraints, and academic progress.

4. **Transparency and independent oversight**—clear grievance routes, unannounced inspections, and published outcomes. Given the industry's track record, trust must be earned, not assumed.

At Northwood, when adults pinned me to the floor, the lesson wasn't "behave." The lesson was **you're not safe here**. Safety is the soil where behavior grows. Without it, everything else is just concrete.

Evidence snapshot

- **Corporal punishment & harsh discipline**: AAP states corporal punishment in schools is ineffective, unethical, and harmful; recommends alternatives.

- **Restraint & seclusion**: U.S. Dept. of Education's 15 principles: never for discipline; only for imminent danger; discontinue ASAP; train staff; notify parents. Recent federal data show stark disability disparities in who is restrained/secluded.

- **"Get-tough" programs**: GAO documented thousands of abuse allegations (including deaths) in private residential/boot-camp programs; Campbell review finds *Scared Straight* increases offending; multi-site evaluations conclude juvenile boot camps do not reduce crime.

- **Trauma & learning**: ACEs are common and tied to mental health and learning/behavior impacts.

- **What works**: PBIS reduces punitive discipline and is evidence-based; trauma-informed school programs and therapies like TF-CBT, PCIT, and MST improve outcomes.

- **Nuance on "military-style"**: The National Guard Youth ChalleNGe Program—voluntary and education-focused—has strong evidence for improving educational outcomes (not a substitute for trauma treatment).

Sports – Where Pain Became Power

Then football found me.

The field was the first place the monster inside made sense. When I strapped on pads and laced my cleats, there was direction for the rage that otherwise had no outlet.

My breakout came during a tackling drill. A kid twice my size squared off across from me. When the whistle blew, I launched. I flattened him. Silence—then roar. Coach's shout, teammates' slaps on the helmet. For the first time, the thing that always got me punished at home earned me applause.

That applause got in my blood. Coaches called me gritty. Teammates said I was hungry. I called it survival. The field, for all its bruises, was a sanctuary. But the wound that fueled me never healed; it just showed on a scoreboard.

This is one of the most important messages—one of the core prongs—of this book. Let your kids play every sport they can. There are lifelong assets, lessons, and self-worth that come from being part of a team. Sports teach accountability, leadership, how to lose with dignity and win with respect. Those lessons 100% bridge into life, work, and relationships.

Get the kids off the phones, out of their rooms, and back outside—on the field, on the court, in the game. They need it. They want it, even if they don't know how to ask for it. Structure gives them a sense of belonging, and belonging can save a life. It saved mine.

Halloween Escape — Starship Earth

If football was the altar, Starship Earth was the sanctuary.

I started working there at ten or eleven. The shop smelled like latex, old glue, and fake blood. Masks hung like severed heads. Steve Urban, the owner, was chaos in human form—he taught me sleight of hand, how to sell fear, how to make people laugh at their own screams. He let me crash at his house when home was unbearable, and he took me to Browns games where his wild laughter drowned out my world.

This was an important stage in my life. The gore and the magic were my daily escape from reality. I think it, at times, saved me from spiraling out of total control. I laughed every day and lost track of time. I made good money and even bartered my pay for the best magic tricks a kid could get his hands on. I had doves that shot flames, sword-in-human-box illusions—the whole act. I even got hired to perform at birthday parties. It was insane, but it was my escape plan, literally. Every trick, every prop, was a piece of freedom I was buying for myself.

I spent so much time with Steve that he started to feel like a second father. He talked to me about life—about choices, about mistakes, about finding humor even when you're hurting. My dad couldn't handle that. He got jealous, angry even. He used to say things like, "Why's he always got little boys hanging around his shop?" and hinted that Steve was some kind of predator. He wasn't. That was just my dad's insecurity talking—he couldn't stand that another man cared about us without an agenda.

We were safe in that crazy world Steve created. He was like a big kid who never grew up, and his joy was contagious. And yeah—it didn't hurt that his wife was an absolute ten.

Through Steve, I met real makeup artists and special effects legends. I'll never forget watching one of them—right there in Cleveland Heights—craft a Freddy Krueger mask by hand. I was hypnotized. That was the day I realized how much artistry and imagination could exist in darkness.

Those were great memories, and to this day, they remain part of my healing. In a time when I was drowning in chaos, that little shop of monsters, masks, and laughter became the safest place I knew.

The Shape of Trust — Chris and the Truth

Those failures taught me not to trust. One person broke that wall—my best friend, Chris.

Chris doesn't coddle. He calls me on my shit. The night he picked me up from jail after I hit my wife in a drunk rage, he didn't excuse me. He looked me dead in the eyes and said, "I expect better from you. What's going on?" No sermon. No pity. Just a mirror I couldn't look away from. That moment didn't let me slip into shame or swagger; it forced me into honesty.

That's the rarest kind of friendship—steady and true. He earned my love not by softness but by showing up and telling the truth. I'll go deeper into our history later, because he's been a pillar in my life for a long time. But here's what matters right now: for a kid who grew up learning not to trust, a friend like Chris is the difference between staying lost and finding a way home.

When you're young and already in trouble, you get good at armor. I wore mine loud. I think Chris sometimes saw me as cocky. He watched me chase status—money, women, the next rush—and maybe he wondered if he should want more out of his own life. Little did he know I wanted what he had: a clean conscience, a safe life, a quiet kind of confidence you can't buy. I didn't want his things; I wanted his center.

Why a true friend matters for troubled youth

A real friend is not a fan club or a fixer. A real friend is structure, truth, and presence. For kids (and former kids) who've learned to expect abandonment, that combination is medicine. Here's what it looks like in practice:

- **Consistency over intensity.** Show up, repeatedly. Keep your word. Trust grows by repetition, not by one heroic gesture.

- **Honesty without humiliation.** Say the hard thing plainly, then stay in the room. Truth that doesn't turn away heals.

- **Boundaries that protect, not punish.** "I love you, and I won't lie for you." That line saves lives.

- **Expectations with belief.** Hold a high bar—*and* believe the person can clear it. Standards without contempt.

- **Modeling a different script.** Live a life that makes better choices imaginable. People copy what they can see.

- **Practical help, not rescue.** Rides, introductions, a couch for a night—support that strengthens, not enables.

- **Celebrate small wins.** Progress sticks when it's noticed. A text—"Proud of you for making that call"—can keep someone going.

Chris did each of those things. He'd check in and then actually show up. He'd tell me "no" when I wanted a shortcut, and "yes" when I needed a hand. He invited me into ordinary, healthy routines—meals that ended without drama, weekends without chaos—until "normal" wasn't a threat anymore. He never excused what I did. He never confused love with covering for me. He held my story, not my excuses.

Trust didn't arrive in a speech. It formed in a thousand simple turns: a call answered, a promise kept, a hard truth said kindly, a boundary held firmly. Over time, the shape of trust came into focus—predictable, strong, and safe enough for me to set the armor down.

I own my actions. There's no justification in this story. Chris wasn't my savior; he was three things I didn't know I needed:

- **A mirror**—so I couldn't lie to myself.

- **A map**—so another way was visible.

- **Some muscle**—when the weight of changing felt too heavy to lift alone.

If you're mentoring, parenting, coaching—or just trying to be that kind of friend—start here: pick consistency over charisma, ask real questions ("What's your plan between now and Friday?"), and keep both your boundaries and your hope. It's not glamorous. It's better. It lasts.

To this day, Chris reminds me there are good people left. He believed I could be one of them long before I did. That's the shape of trust in my life—the steady outline of a friend who told me the truth and stayed.

Final Reflection

As I write this, tears blur the page. I finally understand why my therapist said this book could be my last step toward closure. I almost ignored that advice. Staying in my box felt safer—even as it suffocated me. But I listened. I am not an author; this wasn't a hobby. This was a drill in survival. I wrote anyway.

Because I wrote, I walk lighter. My body—clenched for more than fifty years—has started to let go. The breath I just took felt like spitting out a ten-pound weight I've carried since childhood.

The system logged their visits and drove away. Teachers praised my reading comprehension but ignored my bruises. Psychologists measured my IQ but missed my fear. I hid in work, in football, in haunted houses, and in hustle. I built out of chaos because building kept me alive.

But none of it erases the worst parts. The boy I slammed on the concrete still haunts me. That fight is proof that damage left untreated becomes contagious.

This is why we sometimes have to take advice and live outside our box. Trauma teaches isolation; advice is the handrail we use to climb out. Someone else's words can open a door we can't find alone. My therapist's push didn't make the past disappear, but it gave me a way through it—page by page, breath by breath.

If you're living through this now—scared, silent, waiting for someone to notice—don't. Tell someone. Keep telling until someone hears. Step outside the box they put you in, or the one you built to survive. Leaving is terrifying. Staying will cost you everything.

Silence will not save you. It didn't save me. It never will.

A Psychologist's Perspective

From a clinical standpoint, this chapter reveals the long-term impact of chronic childhood trauma—particularly when it goes unacknowledged or dismissed by those who should protect or intervene.

Repeated exposure to abuse, coupled with systemic neglect, often creates what's known as complex post-traumatic stress disorder (C-PTSD). Unlike a single traumatic event, this form of trauma rewires a child's developing brain around survival rather than safety. Every interaction becomes filtered through threat assessment: Is this safe? Will this hurt? Do I need to defend myself or disappear?

The behaviors described—running away, acting out in school, even that explosion of violence—aren't random. They're the body's language when words fail. The child doesn't wake up choosing rebellion; the nervous system is choosing defense. When safety is inconsistent, control becomes oxygen. Even chaos feels familiar, and therefore, safer than uncertainty.

The dog's loyalty, the obsession with Halloween, the discipline of football—all became adaptive survival mechanisms. They were ways to anchor identity in environments that stripped it away. These "escapes" were not weakness or distraction; they were lifelines. In therapy, we often call these protective parts—pieces of the self that learn to hold the pain so the person can keep functioning.

The adult who emerges from such experiences is often driven, hyper-vigilant, deeply loyal, and at times emotionally avoidant. These traits—though forged in trauma—can become strengths once understood and integrated. Healing comes when survival stops being the only goal and connection becomes safe again.

The message here for parents, teachers, and professionals is simple but critical: look beyond behavior. Every "problem child" has a reason. The earlier we listen to what the behavior is trying to say, the more lives we save—not just from pain, but from silence.

Small Action Steps (If You're Living This Now)

- Tell one safe person—teacher, coach, counselor—today. Keep trying until someone listens.

- Write down dates and details and store them somewhere safe.

- Find one outlet—sport, art, music—that lets the energy move instead of explode.

- If therapy isn't possible, reach out to local youth services or a crisis line.

- Parents: if your child's grades fall off a cliff, investigate what's happening at home before you write it off as laziness.

Silence will not save you. It didn't save me. It never will.

Chapter 3:
A Ride That Saved My Life

"I missed the bus—but destiny pulled over."

There's a moment in every survivor's story when the tide shifts—when pain meets purpose, and chaos meets a calling. For me, it all started with a missed bus.

I was in sixth grade at Roxboro Middle School in Cleveland Heights. Normally, I walked home with friends—talking trash, throwing snowballs, clowning around. That long, 40-minute walk was a stretch of freedom, a sacred space between the fake safety of school and the very real hell waiting at home.

At school, I wore a mask. I laughed loud. I cracked jokes. I walked with a bounce I didn't feel. I had to—the other option was letting the world see how broken I really was. Back then, you didn't talk about things like trauma. You didn't say, "My brother hits me, and sexually assaults me. My dad drinks and rages. My mother regrets having me." You just survived.

One random day, I decided to take the bus instead of walking. I don't know why. Maybe I just didn't want to be around people. Maybe I was already spiraling inside. I took too long at my locker, missed the bus, missed my friends, missed every ride.

And I stood there on the sidewalk, alone. Silent. And then a Jeep pulled up.

It was loud, bright, lifted, and unforgettable. The guy behind the wheel looked like he stepped out of a Whitesnake video—flowing hair, Ray-Bans, and that effortless 80s cool. He smiled at me like I wasn't invisible.

"Hop in," he said. "I want to talk to you." And I did.

In that moment, I didn't care if he was a stranger. I would've gotten in anyone's car just to avoid the walk back to pain. But he wasn't just anyone. He was Coach Jarvie.

He told me about football. About tryouts. Said I had potential. Me. No one had used that word around me before.

All my life, I've gone back to that ride—the fork in the road, the split-second choice that flashed like fire and blew open a lifetime of doors. It still feels surreal that one turn could reroute everything. I thank God for that day.

I went to preseason conditioning. I started lifting weights more seriously—something I'd dabbled in with Grandpa Ray out at Venice Beach during summer visits. I thought I was Billy Badass… until the first day in pads.

I walked into a locker room full of mostly Black kids, bigger than me, louder than me. Some looked like they already had kids of their own. They joked, pushed, shouted. I was terrified.

And then I met "House."

House was 6'4", probably 350 pounds. A damn mountain. First hitting drill, I lined up across from him. He ate me alive. I thought about quitting.

That night, my dad—already drunk by 7PM—asked how practice went.

"I'm quitting," I told him. "I'm no good. House kicked my ass."

He told me to get into my stance.

Then he shoved me so hard I flew backward into the brick fireplace wall.

I cried.

"Did that hurt?" he asked.

"Yes," I said.

"Nobody will ever hit you harder than that."

And you know what? He was right.

Next day at practice, I squared off with House again. This time, I locked up, held my ground, didn't get blown off the ball.

Something changed that day.

I got stronger. I started driving people off the ball. I stopped flinching. I started rising.

Sixth through eighth grade, I got better and better. By our eighth grade team party, private schools like Benedictine and St. Ignatius were already scouting me. Everyone knew I was a physical player. Crazy even.

But my anger wasn't just football toughness.

I was suspended over 20 times for fighting. I beat kids senseless just for looking at me wrong. I carried every insult from home like a time bomb in my gut. My mom told me she wished she'd had an abortion. My brother beat and molested me. My dad was a drunk tyrant.

The only time I stayed out of trouble and kept good grades was during football season. I was legally allowed to be violent—and people cheered.

And then came the rug pull.

I was supposed to go to Cleveland Heights High. I stayed local to be with the guys I grew close to walking home from Roxboro. Roxboro was home of the Rockets—the worst logo ever, like some hand-drawn future spaceman.

Coach Kerry Hodakievic drove me to two-a-days. It felt like Coach Jarvie all over again—safe, known, protected.

I made the starting lineup as a freshman. Special teams. Blocking back for Van Ward, one of the best running backs in the state. I was in heaven.

And then I came home one day and heard, "Pack up. We're moving."

"Why?" I asked.

"Taxes are too high."

"Dad's drive is too long."

And then there was the scrimmage against Shaw. Lights out mid-game. Fights in the stands. Someone got stabbed and shot outside, we were told. The Lake Erie League moved our games from Friday nights to daylight hours.

And just like that, my world was boxed up and hauled away…

To Brunswick.

I didn't even know where that was.

It felt like exile. It felt like a punishment.

But sometimes a setback is a setup for something greater.

We left without goodbyes. At fourteen that felt like a theft—of proof that I mattered to anyone outside my front door. One day I had a bus stop, a lunch table, a kid who saved me a seat. The next day I had a forwarding address and a knot in my stomach. No ritual, no last hangout, no "see you around." Just gone. The grief didn't have a place to land, so it settled in me.

Being the new kid with low confidence is its own kind of camouflage. I learned the hallway map before I learned names. I watched how people laughed so I could time mine a half-second behind. I kept my backpack on both shoulders, zipper up, eyes down. If you don't announce yourself, no one can reject you—that was the logic. On the outside I tried on whatever costume seemed safest: quiet, funny, tough. Inside I felt small and breakable.

School became survival first, learning second. By the time the bell rang I'd already spent all my energy scanning for where to sit, who to avoid, how to not look lost. Algebra didn't have a chance. Teachers read the distance as attitude, or the fidgeting as disrespect. I wasn't trying to be a problem. I was trying to not be a target. When you don't believe you belong, it's easier to fail on purpose than to risk failing after trying.

The move trained me not to attach. I started ending things before they began—sports I might have loved, friendships that felt too close, chances that asked for effort. If I left first, I couldn't be left. I stopped decorating rooms. I kept answers short when people asked where I was from. I practiced disappearing as a skill.

The longer-term impact was quieter but heavier: I carried a permanent new-kid feeling into places where I wasn't new anymore.

Even when people offered me a seat, I stood. Even when teachers were kind, I waited for the other shoe. Leaving without goodbye taught me speed and caution. It took much longer to learn trust, to believe that some people stay, and that I didn't have to stay ready to run.

Psychologist's Perspective: Understanding the Hidden Wounds

From a clinical standpoint, the experiences described in this chapter reflect complex trauma—trauma that is layered, repeated, and often inflicted by those closest to the child. When abuse is physical, sexual, emotional, and environmental all at once, the nervous system adapts by entering survival mode. Over time, this hypervigilance becomes the norm. Children learn to anticipate threats, shut down emotionally, or explode violently—not because they are broken, but because it is how their brain keeps them safe.

This story also highlights a well-documented psychological coping strategy called "compartmentalization." The ability to excel in football while navigating a war zone at home is a survival mechanism. It's what allows trauma survivors to function in one arena while falling apart in another. For many, sports become the one safe outlet where aggression is not only permitted but celebrated.

Furthermore, the attachment to mentors like Coach Jarvie and Coach Hodakievic is critical. In psychology, we call this "corrective emotional experiences." These relationships offered stability, belief, and structure—things absent at home. They become essential stepping stones to recovery, self-worth, and eventual healing.

The emotional volatility described—fighting, suspensions, rage—are not character flaws. They are symptoms. Symptoms of unresolved trauma, abandonment, and betrayal. What this chapter shows is not just how trauma destroys—but how something as simple as a ride, a whistle, or a coach's belief can become the catalyst for transformation.

Self-Help & Advice: Turning Pain into Power

Your Pain is Valid—But It Doesn't Get to Lead Forever

You have every right to be angry. Every right to be exhausted. What happened to you was real. But your trauma doesn't get to drive anymore. Recognize it, speak it, and then slowly start giving it less control over your decisions.

🏈 Try This: Write one sentence that used to define you—then rewrite it into one that empowers you. Example:
"I was abused." → "I survived abuse—and I'm still here building something better."

Accept the Help—Even if it Feels Uncomfortable

That Jeep? That coach? That ride? I could've turned it down. I could've let pride or fear shut the door. But sometimes life sends you rescue in a form you didn't expect. Be open. Don't assume everyone is out to hurt you.

🏈 Try This: When someone offers help—pause before you reject it. Ask yourself: "What if this is the moment that changes everything?"

Channel Your Rage into Craft, Not Chaos

Football gave me a safe, structured place to release all the violence, fear, and anger I carried. Your version of football might be something else—music, art, business, working with your hands, mentoring others. Find your outlet and get obsessed.

🛠 Try This: Ask yourself, "What activity makes me feel strong, focused, or calm?" Do it daily. Make it your medicine. Master it over time.

Consistency Beats Confidence

I didn't believe in myself when I started. But I showed up. I lifted the weights. I stood back up after getting hit. You don't need to feel brave every day—just committed. The rest comes.

🛠 Try This: Set a daily routine you can control—waking up, reading, journaling, working out. Keep the promise to yourself even when life gets hard. Especially then.

Momentum is Fragile—Protect It with Everything You've Got

One decision, one move, one distraction can steal the progress you worked so hard to build. When you're gaining ground—guard it. Focus. Don't get too comfortable.

🛠 Try This: Write down what's working in your life right now. Circle it. Protect it. Make decisions around keeping that momentum alive.

You may not have chosen your childhood. But you get to choose your adulthood. And no matter how broken it feels—you're not alone. There's always another bus. Another coach. Another chance to start again.

You just have to stay open… and keep walking toward it.

Chapter 4:
Friday Nights & Father Figures

"Between the hash marks, I found my worth."

Friday nights had a pulse. The stadium lights hummed like electric suns. The air carried the sting of autumn—fresh-cut grass, grilled hot dogs, and adrenaline sharp enough to taste. For most kids, football was recreation. For me, it was redemption.

I'd walk out of the tunnel, helmet in hand, staring at that field like it was a church. Between those white chalk lines, my past couldn't chase me. The chaos of home couldn't reach me. The field didn't care about my last name, my bruises, or my broken nights—it only cared about one thing: effort.

Here, the scoreboard told the truth. You earned everything you got.

My First Father Figures

My coaches didn't just blow whistles—they breathed life into me. At home, "discipline" meant fear. On the field, it meant preparation. When Coach barked, "Run it again," it wasn't cruelty—it was belief.

For the first time, I had men who meant what they said. No broken promises. No lies. If you gave effort, they gave back. It was that simple. Life at home was chaos, but football had order, logic, and fairness. I studied those men—how they carried themselves, how they commanded a room, how their word meant something. They weren't perfect, but they were steady, and to a boy like me, steadiness was oxygen.

These were real men. Tough, loud, brutally honest, and unflinching. They didn't sugarcoat life—they prepared you for it. Looking back, I think someone was paying it forward. Maybe one of their own coaches, or one of their mentors, had told them to keep an eye out for the broken ones like me.

That's something I'll cover later in this book—when I became a coach myself at my old school. Because I now understand what they were doing. They were shaping boys into men. And in a way, they were healing something inside themselves while doing it.

See, my theory is simple: you don't play football if you're normal.

Running full speed, headfirst, into another strong, fast, built man for fun isn't for the faint of heart. You have to be a little off—edgy, scarred, or broken in some way. I don't care what anyone says, there's something ticking inside football players. Something that makes us crave that hit, that contact, that moment of chaos where the world finally makes sense.

Maybe that's why I loved it so much. Because for once, the pain had a purpose.

Brotherhood in the Locker Room

We weren't just teammates—we were a band of outcasts, dreamers, and fighters who somehow made each other whole. Some had perfect parents and clean homes. Others came from bruises and broken glass like me. But when we suited up, we were equal.

We taped each other's ankles, traded jokes to hide nerves, and fought side by side every Friday night under the lights. The locker room was a second home. After a win, it thundered with helmet slaps and victory roars. After a loss, silence felt heavy—mutual pain, mutual respect.

Football taught me the unspoken code of real brotherhood: you never let your teammate fight alone. That lesson carried me through life long after the pads came off.

And to this day—decades later—at every phase of my football career, from middle school to the pros—I still have contact and connection with former teammates. Those bonds never broke. We've grown older, built families, started careers, but when we talk, it's like we're still in that locker room, still kids chasing the same dream.

It's an unbreakable bond—one that time, distance, or circumstance could never touch.

The Move That Broke Me

Leaving Cleveland Heights meant leaving my team, my coaches, and the only place I'd ever felt safe. I was being ripped away from my brotherhood and dropped into a town I didn't understand.

When I showed up in Brunswick, I was the new kid—the loud kid from Cleveland. I had no friends, just football, and I was determined not to start over at the bottom.

But the first few weeks of camp were rough. I looked around and didn't see a single familiar face—or a hint of diversity. Everyone was pink or pale, same haircut, same accent, same playlists. I remember thinking, we are so fucked.

We had some absolute beasts on the line—big, strong farm-fed guys—but no real game-breakers. No speed. No one who looked like the kind of athlete I was used to playing with at Cleveland Heights. That place was a melting pot—different backgrounds, sounds, and styles. Brunswick felt sterile, like football in black and white.

Then one afternoon, everything changed.

A week or so before our first game, I heard this southern drawl from behind me during warm-ups. It stopped me cold. That wasn't an Ohio accent. I turned around and saw him—Demetrius "D-Mac."

Zero body fat, pure muscle, and speed that looked like it came out of a track lab. His presence alone felt like color had finally been painted back into the picture. I remember thinking, finally—someone who gets it.

From day one, we connected. He wasn't from around there either, and I think he saw the same thing in me—a kindred spirit in a place that felt too clean, too careful. D-Mac had that same chip, that same hunger. And when he ran, he was poetry in motion.

I loved blocking for that kid. He made every hole I opened look like a highlight reel. When he crossed the goal line, it felt like I scored too. He was the missing piece of home I didn't know I needed.

Cleveland Heights had culture. Brunswick had structure—but no soul. D-Mac brought a heartbeat to that team. And for the first time, I didn't feel like an outsider. I felt like we had a fighting chance.

Brunstucky Baptism: Standing My Ground

The seniors didn't take kindly to me. To them, I was an outsider, a threat, a mouth that needed shut. They tried to haze me, to put me in my place.

"Carry our gear," one said. "Crawl through the mud, rookie."

I looked him dead in the eye. "Hell no. Fuck you."

That's all it took. Helmets dropped. The locker room exploded. I was surrounded, ready to be jumped, but I didn't back down. I'd taken worse beatings in my own home. I wasn't scared.

Then, out of nowhere, a mountain of a kid stepped in—Chris DiFranco. Built like an oak tree, strong as hell. He threw himself between me and the crowd and said, "Not today."

That was the end of it.

That day, I earned their respect the hard way. And Chris? He became my brother. Turns out, he was from Cleveland too—another outsider in "Brunstucky." We bonded instantly. From that day on, if someone came for one of us, they had to go through both of us.

But that respect wasn't fully cemented until the first big test.

These same guys who had tried to haze me got front-row seats to my coming-out party. One Friday night, I stepped in against one of the best linebackers in the country—this dude had Division I offers from everywhere. He was a senior, and I was just a sophomore. I'd read about him in the papers, heard the hype, and yeah—I was terrified.

First snap—boom. Met him head-on, drove him backward. Second snap, same thing. By the third, he was shaking his head in disbelief. I owned him.

By halftime, my teammates were slapping my helmet, yelling, "Dude, you're fucking killing it!" My tailback ran back after a long gain and shouted, "Bro, the holes are huge—nobody's touching me!"

That night, I arrived.

The arrogance I carried wasn't born out of ego—it was survival finally rewarded. For once, all the pain, anger, and grit inside me had somewhere to go. Respect carried over year after year after that performance.

I wasn't the new kid anymore. I was the kid you didn't mess with.

Summer Sweat and Stairway to Glory

That summer before the season, we lived and breathed football. All summer long, and all week before the games, we ran the stadium stairs in the blistering heat—the kind that stuck to your skin like glue and burned through your lungs like fire.

We didn't need a crowd to motivate us—there wasn't one anyway. We worked when no one was watching. When the stands were empty and the air smelled like cut grass and asphalt. We chased exhaustion like it owed us something.

We were insane in the best way. There were days we'd eat grass after sprints, just for the hell of it, daring each other to one-up the crazy. We even started jokingly praying to Vince Lombardi—the "football god" himself. Yep, true story.

We built our own religion out of sweat, pain, and competition. That's how deep it went for us. It wasn't a game anymore—it was identity.

The Tunnel Vision of War

Once the lights came on Friday nights, everything changed. People always talk about hearing the roar of the crowd, but for me, it was silent. Once I put that helmet on, the world muted.

It was like an out-of-body experience—slow motion, tunnel vision. Every sound was muffled, every heartbeat drawn out. I was high on adrenaline, six Advils deep, and, truth be told, juiced up on whatever I thought would make me faster or stronger—black beauties, speed pills, even roids during a few of those years.

Everything slowed down like an old movie reel.

I'd lock eyes with the opposing line and talk endless shit. Called out defenders by name before the snap, daring them to stop me. Half the time, I didn't even remember what I said; it was instinct, rage, and belief that I was untouchable.

And somehow—it worked.

When you're that far inside the game, when your mind and body blend into one chaotic machine, pain becomes irrelevant. You stop thinking. You just hit, move, win.

But looking back, I realize how destructive that mindset was. I wasn't chasing glory—I was running from pain. The hits, the fights, the pressure—it numbed everything else.

The Season That Almost Never Happened

I wasn't even supposed to play football my senior year. During my physical, the doctor paused mid-exam, his expression tightening as he listened to my heartbeat. He heard something—an irregular rhythm.

A heart murmur.

It wasn't the first time someone had mentioned it. When I was younger, doctors thought I'd outgrow it. And for years, I passed every sports physical without issue. But that year—the most important year of my life—it came back.

The doctor said he couldn't clear me until I saw a specialist for an ultrasound. The next available appointment? Late October. By then, the season would be over.

It felt like my entire world collapsed in one breath. Football wasn't just a game—it was my identity, my ticket to college, and maybe my only shot out of the chaos I was born into. Without it, I had no direction.

That morning, I still went to the gym before sunrise, lifting like a man trying to outrun fate. But every rep felt heavier than usual—not from the weight, but from the fear.

And then I made a choice I'm not proud of, but one that changed everything. At 6 a.m., I walked into the trainer's office while the building was still quiet. I went through his desk until I found other players' physical forms. I stole one, took it home, and copied the vitals onto my own blue physical sheet.

Then, I flipped open the phone book—remember those?—and started scanning for a name that could fly under the radar. I landed on "Dr. Chang." There were at least twenty of them listed in the Cleveland area. Perfect.

I forged his signature, turned in my form, and just like that, I was "cleared." The guilt was immediate, but the relief was stronger. Football was back. My future was back.

Later that fall, I finally got the ultrasound. The doctor looked at the screen and smiled. He said, "You've got the strongest heart I've seen in a long time. Your chambers and valves pump nearly twice as hard as the average person's."

I laughed to myself. *Maybe that's why I'm so damn persistent.*

That diagnosis didn't just clear me—it explained me. That drive, that refusal to quit, that constant need to push through pain—it wasn't just psychological. Maybe I was built that way. Maybe I was wired to fight.

But that same season also exposed my flaws—the darker side of that relentless drive.

The Confrontation with Coach Fasko

Coach Fasko, rest his soul, pulled me aside one afternoon. "Anthony," he said, "we need to talk. There are rumors going around—people saying you're using anabolic steroids. Tell me the truth. Are you?"

I didn't hesitate. "Hell no, Coach."

But the truth? I had just jabbed my quad with two CCs minutes before practice. The adrenaline of the lie hit harder than the needle. As I stood there swearing on my reputation, I looked down and saw a small spot of blood soaking through my white game pants from the injection site.

My heart sank. I was lying to a man who genuinely cared about me—not the player, but the person.

The steroids weren't about vanity or performance anymore. They were about control. Every time life spun out, I tried to muscle it back into place. I thought I could bench-press my pain into submission. I was wrong.

Sometimes I was such an arrogant asshole to Coach Fasko—cocky, dismissive, reckless. He deserved better from me. He saw potential; I gave him attitude. Years later, I realized that whatever negative things he might've told college recruiters about me, I earned them.

At that point, I was playing like a man possessed—on borrowed time, with a forged signature, an altered body, and a conflicted soul. I was winning battles on the field but losing the war within.

A Familiar Face in a Foreign Land

A week later, during camp, my new coach called me into his office. "Got a surprise for you," he said.

I walked in and froze. Sitting there in a Brunswick polo was my old Cleveland Heights coach, Coach McPhie.

He looked up and smirked. "Hey, dummy."

Just like that, a piece of home had followed me.

McPhie was tough—never one to hand out compliments. He chewed you out when you missed a block, glared when you fumbled, and walked away if you tried to make excuses. But what I didn't realize at the time was that he saw through me. He knew I didn't need coddling—I needed someone to hold me accountable, to channel my anger into something constructive.

Every insult was a challenge. Every criticism was fuel. He pushed me harder than anyone because he knew I could take it. And deep down, I loved him for it.

The Night I Finally Broke

Fast-forward to senior year. The season had ended, and we were at the awards banquet. I sat there half-listening, assuming I wouldn't be mentioned. McPhie had never given me a single compliment—not once.

Then he took the microphone.

He started talking about one of the hardest-working players he'd ever coached. Said it was an honor to coach this kid. That he gave his all, every day, and never quit.

Before calling my name, he said, "Lurpavich, come up here."

Now, this man had called me that nickname for years, and one day I finally asked, "Coach, what the hell is a Lurpavich?"

Without missing a beat, he said, "It's a man who smells little girls' bicycle seats."

To this day, I still don't know if that's a real German word—Google sure hasn't helped. But that was Coach McPhie. Old-school. Rough around the edges. No filters, no apologies.

Back then, we laughed hard. Nobody got offended. We could take a joke, even when it stung a little, because we knew the intent behind it. That locker-room humor, as raw as it was, built toughness. It was his way of saying, You're one of us now.

He looked out at the crowd and said, "You're raising men here, not boys."

Then he said my real name.

"Anthony Hodel, come up here."

He held up a plaque and said, "Hardest-working kid I ever coached."

The room clapped, and something inside me cracked open. The tears came before I could stop them. For a kid who'd never once heard "I'm proud of you" from a father figure, that moment broke me in the best way possible.

That night, I realized tough love is still love. Sometimes, the ones who push you the hardest are the ones who see your potential the clearest.

A Psychologist's Perspective: The Healing Power of Structure and Brotherhood

From a clinical standpoint, what happened on that field wasn't just athletic—it was therapeutic. Psychologists often call it "functional discipline"—the idea that external structure can help regulate internal chaos. For kids from unstable homes, like I was, structure doesn't restrict; it heals.

Football provided that structure. Every whistle, every drill, every repetition became a ritual that rewired my nervous system. Trauma thrives in unpredictability, but football is predictable. The playbook doesn't change overnight. The cadence is consistent. When life outside the locker room was chaos, the game offered safety through repetition.

There's also something profoundly psychological about brotherhood. According to research in trauma recovery, belonging and connection are two of the most effective protectors against long-term emotional damage. I didn't need therapy at that age—I needed a team. The locker room became my group session. The field was my stage to reframe pain into purpose.

Even the so-called "tough love" from coaches played a role in rewiring my sense of authority. For a child whose earliest authority figures caused fear or harm, a coach who demands excellence but means well can change everything. It introduces a new model of leadership—one based on respect, accountability, and growth instead of fear.

Psychologically, football replaced my trauma triggers with performance triggers. Instead of reacting to anger or fear, I learned to channel those emotions into focus and physical action. The adrenaline that once fueled rage now fueled determination.

In essence, football was exposure therapy with a scoreboard. It helped me rebuild trust, regulate emotion, and develop self-worth—all under the guise of a game.

And while I didn't realize it then, that brotherhood and discipline laid the groundwork for my adult healing. It showed me that even broken boys can rebuild their wiring when given structure, belief, and a team that refuses to let them fall.

Self-Help & Advice Section: Lessons Between the Hash Marks

1. Structure Saves You – When your world feels chaotic, build a schedule. Routine becomes a safety net for your mind.
2. Brotherhood Beats Isolation – Find your team. Surround yourself with people who challenge and protect you.
3. Tough Love Is Still Love – The people who push you the hardest often care the most.
4. Earn Respect, Don't Demand It – Titles mean nothing without effort.
5. Pain Isn't the Enemy—Stagnation Is – Growth hurts, but staying the same hurts worse.
6. Be the Coach You Needed – Guide others through their chaos with patience and empathy.
7. Control the Noise – Focus on the play in front of you, not the voices in the stands.
8. Keep Your Helmet On – Protect your mindset; you'll take hits you never see coming.
9. Don't Just Win—Evolve – Let success refine you, not define you.

Closing Reflection

When I left Cleveland Heights, I thought my dream was over. The transfer papers felt like a verdict, and "Brunstucky" sounded less like a town and more like a warning. But that move—to Brunswick—became the test that defined me.

I learned how to fight for respect when nobody knew my name. How to lead without waiting for permission slips or titles. How to take anger—the kind that buzzes in your jaw—and turn it into quiet, repeatable work. Early lifts when the sky was still gray. Bus rides where you replayed mistakes until they stung a little less. Last reps when lungs burned and excuses tried to bargain. That's where I started trading frustration for discipline, and noise for focus.

Football gave me my first family: coaches who demanded more than I thought I had, teammates who didn't care about my zip code as long as I showed up on time and finished the drill. Brunswick tested me. It also crowned me. Between those two truths lived the hard parts: the locker-room confrontations, the days my confidence wobbled, the practices where I had to choose between pride and progress. The crown didn't come from a single play; it came from staying when quitting would've been easier.

From fighting in locker rooms to standing on that banquet stage, I learned the rule that never changes: the world won't hand you validation—you earn it with blood, sweat, and belief. And when Coach McPhie called me to that stage, something shifted. I realized I wasn't just collecting father figures; I was becoming one for myself. I had built a voice I could trust, a standard I could live by, a compass that didn't panic when the map changed.

I can point to the scars and tell you what each one taught me: how to speak when it matters, how to be quiet when it counts, how to show up for others even when the spotlight is pointed elsewhere. Leadership, I learned, isn't loud. It's consistent. It's the extra film session. It's the apology after a bad moment. It's making sure the freshman who looks lost finds his group before practice starts.

So, when I say Brunswick crowned me, I don't mean trophies. I mean ownership. I mean walking into rooms without shrinking. I mean being strong enough to carry weight and wise enough to share it. The field taught me effort; life taught me stewardship.

Between the hash marks, I found my worth. Beyond them, I discovered my purpose.

Anthony James Hodel

Chapter 5:
Muscle, Mayhem & Mexico

"At 15, I wasn't selling drugs—I was trafficking power."

Iron Temples and Broken Boys

The first time I touched a weight, it felt like I was holding onto something real. Something I could control. A cold bar of steel was more dependable than anything I had at home. That bar didn't yell at me. It didn't hit me. It didn't lie. It just waited. And I showed up. Every day.

Cleveland Heights YMCA. The school weight room. Alta House in Little Italy.

I didn't go home after school—not because I didn't have a home, but because what was waiting there wasn't home at all. The gym was the only place I wasn't being screamed at, belittled, or abused. The clang of the weights was louder than the yelling in my head. I could outlift my trauma—at least, I thought I could.

Chris and I drew our bond closer in the weight room, building each other physically and mentally. He was my brother—I spent more time with him than my own family. I'll never forget how his parents opened their home up to me. One night, I ate the whole family dinner thinking it was just an appetizer. I swear I ate 30 chicken tenders. Ms. D hit me with a broom, pissed as all hell. "Guess we gotta order pizza?" she said. I practically lived there—it was safe. Chris and I did epic, crazy shit—stunts Johnny Knoxville would applaud. We still laugh about it to this day.

Knoxville-Worthy Mayhem

Chris was a **guy's guy**—steady, loyal, unflinching—and he always had my back. Junior year, we were working as bouncers at a nightclub. One night, four or five girls I was "seeing" from other schools showed up at the same time. I ducked into the office with one and whispered, "Chris, you gotta cover for me." He just nodded and ran interference like a pro. He didn't judge. He covered. That was Chris.

We did dumb, fearless stuff that still makes my stomach flip. We'd run our cars full speed into the snow mounds behind the school—no exaggeration—ice piled thirty feet high. We hit them like we were testing airbags for a living. We were flat-out insane.

Another night, Chris thought a cop was on our tail. He killed the headlights and punched it—ninety miles an hour down a narrow street, pitch black. I was in the passenger seat, sure we were about to clip a parked car and launch into the void. Somehow, we didn't. He could match my crazy when the moment called for it. To this day, I've never asked him why.

The wildest night burned itself into my memory at a basketball game. Our teammate Rob—**rest his soul**—went up to dunk and got undercut. He flipped vertical, straight over, and came down on his head. One of my dad's best friends lost his son in a high school game to the same kind of play. Something snapped in me. I rushed the court, grabbed the defender—kid was about 6'4"—and in a full-on WWF moment, pile-drove him onto the hardwood.

Chaos detonated. Cops, coaches, students—everyone exploded onto the floor. Chris got held back in the surge; I shouted, "We gotta go!" We bolted, tearing through mall parking lots with sirens on us until we dead-ended down a one-way alley and met a brick wall. I tried to climb it like it was going to open a door. It didn't. They threw us into the back of the cruiser together, and we sat there laughing like idiots—adrenaline drunk, young, and reckless.

I could fill a book with the crazy things we did. None of it is a boast. We crossed lines. We made bad choices. But here's the truth: no matter how crazy it got, I felt **safe** with Chris. He was a human anchor in a life that kept trying to toss me overboard.

Bottom line? Let boys be boys. Let them mess up. Let them find their edges. That's where the stories are born. That's where the healing starts.

New Zip Code, Same Demons

When I got pulled from Cleveland Heights and dumped in Brunswick, it felt like being exiled to another planet. Gone were my teammates, my people, my rhythm. Now I was just a kid with pain in his chest and rage in his knuckles, trying to adapt in a strange town filled with strange faces.

But like always, I found a way. I sniffed out the gym—the sanctuary.

It wasn't long before I fell in with the older guys. Some were two years ahead of me. Some ten. Most of them were stacked like Greek gods and moved like they owned the room. I trained like a machine to keep up. Hell, I didn't just want to be accepted—I wanted to be respected.

Every guy in there was juiced to the gills. I mean everyone. Even one of the women walked around at 190 pounds of lean, ripped muscle. That wasn't dedication. That was chemistry.

But to me, it wasn't cheating. It was a roadmap. I didn't see steroids as a drug—I saw them as the fast track out of my pain. Out of my powerlessness. Out of me.

This is where Chris and I had a degree of separation. He never cheated, lied, or took a shortcut. He was against it. His family knew what I was doing and questioned him about his choice in a close friend. They even asked if I was selling drugs. He knew me. He knew I never sold anything. He had my back. But today, I think he was concerned about the darkness I was entering.

Meeting Big Mike

I'll never forget the first conversation I had with Big Mike. Dude was massive. Traps for days. Forearms like ham hocks. He had this dead yellow tint in his eyes—the color of old corn. Jaundice, I later learned.

He told me about Anadrol 50. Ten weeks later, I put on 35 pounds of muscle. I wasn't a scared kid anymore. I was a machine.

What I didn't have words for then was *why* it hit so hard. A therapist would later call it muscle dysmorphia—a form of Body Dysmorphic Disorder. In my head, the mirror was a funhouse that only bent one way: no matter how big I got, it shaved off twenty pounds. Compliments slid off me. Progress looked like failure with better lighting. The goalposts moved every time I got close. "Bigger" wasn't a target; it was a horizon.

Steroids didn't just add size; they answered that distortion on every channel. Chemically, they turned the volume up—energy spiked, appetite roared, workouts felt electric. The pump wasn't just blood; it was relief. My brain lit up on certainty: **this** is working. Psychologically, the armor was instant. Strangers stepped aside.

Bouncers nodded me in. Shirts fit like I'd earned a new last name. Every look of respect (or fear) was another stamp that said *you are finally enough*—and BDD kept whispering back, *almost*. Socially, I plugged into a tribe: routines, rituals, inside language. Pin day, meal prep, macros—discipline masquerading as recovery, and the crew cheering the same chase. Identity-wise, it solved an old problem in a new costume: I wasn't "the kid" anymore; I was the guy you didn't want to mess with. That felt like safety.

And once you ride that loop, coming off isn't neutral—it's loss. Strength dips, fullness fades, the mirror gets mean again. You don't just miss the muscle; you miss the *story* the muscle told about you. So you promise yourself one more cycle to hold the line. BDD loves "one more." It turns maintenance into a cliff edge and calls it self-improvement.

So yeah—I was hooked. Hooked on a chemical buzz that made my body feel like a loaded bar. Hooked on the way people looked at me. Hooked on the ritual that made every day feel on-mission. But most of all, hooked on the quiet that came when the numbers climbed and the mirror shut up for a minute. That's the trap with body dysmorphia: the world rewards your sickness while your brain keeps moving the finish line. Steroids didn't fix the hole. They gave me bigger shoulders to carry it.

Mexico: My First Taste of Freedom—and Fear

I told my parents I was going to Michigan for a football visit. I flew to Mexico.

We trained at Rich Gaspari's gym, saw Anna Nicole Smith during a Guess photoshoot. We thought we were living. And steroids? Everywhere. Pharmacies, corner stores. Paradise.

But it got darker. I started making steroid cocktails—mixing multiple compounds and shooting up just to feel the fibers tear as the oil pushed through deep into the muscle tissue. I was addicted at every level. They did coke. I did more roids.

It was out of control. My parents, my coaches—everyone turned a blind eye. They saw size and performance, not pain and dependency. Nobody asked what I was running from. They just cheered me on.

Smuggling Mayhem

When our order came in—boxes and boxes of steroids—we realized we were in over our heads. So we got creative.

We took long strips of tape and lined the vials up like bullets. We wrapped them around our legs, our stomachs, our backs—until we looked "even." Not bloated. Not suspicious. Just solid. We dumped 50cc bottles of Equipoise into sterilized Paul Mitchell shampoo bottles and buried them deep in our luggage.

Back then, Mexico customs used a red-light/green-light system. Hit green, you walk. Hit red, they tear you apart.

I hit green. Three times.

The Button

Back in the U.S., my 6'4" juiced-up friends walked through customs like it was a grocery store. No questions. No scans. No nerves.

Me? 5'11", taped up like a walking pharmacy?

Buzzer.

They pulled me aside.

I stood there, looking at the posters behind the agent—federal prison sentences, mugshots, confiscated drugs. 15 to 25 years. I thought my life was over. Fifty feet away, I could see my friends laughing. Free men. I was sweating like I'd run a marathon.

The agent scanned me.

Beep. Again. Beep.

"Turn around," he said.

He scanned my waistband.

"Just your shorts button," he chuckled. "You're good to go."

Then he patted me on the back.

Right on the tape.

I walked out into the arrival lane. My dad was the getaway driver.

He looked at me.

"You okay? You look like you just saw a ghost."

I said, "I don't feel good," and puked in his car. I swear I could've shit through a screen for a week from the stress.

And here's the insane part?

I did it two more times.

The Cost of the Mask

In the '90s, steroids weren't considered drugs. You weren't an addict—you were "dedicated." But I was addicted. Fully.

I was no better than any other addict.

I stole. I hustled. I lied. All to make sure I had that pump. That fullness. That illusion of control.

People point fingers at crackheads and meth heads, but addiction has many faces.

Some of them wear tank tops.

Mike Died. I Didn't.

Big Mike didn't make it.

Liver failure. Heart explosion. Take your pick.

I worked as a bouncer at nightclubs. A lot of the guys I juiced with were there, too—standing tall, arms crossed, intimidating every drunk who walked through the door.

And then they started dropping.

Year after year. Heart attacks. One after another. Freaking flies.

I made it to 52. I'm healthy. I've had bloodwork done. I got lucky.

But it wasn't luck. It was distance.

I walked away from the culture. From the guys. From the identity.

Psychologist's Perspective: Power, Pain, and the Pursuit of Control

From a psychological standpoint, this story reflects a trauma-driven need for control. When a child grows up in chaos, the brain becomes hard-wired to crave predictability. The gym—and later, steroids—

became an illusion of order. The weights didn't judge. The results were measurable. The transformation was visible, and for someone who grew up unseen, that visibility felt like love.

But beneath the muscle sat unprocessed pain. Trauma survivors often channel emotional pain into physical exertion because the body becomes a battlefield the mind can't yet enter. Every rep, every injection, every new vein surfacing was rebellion against helplessness.

The body became both armor and prison. The needle replaced the abuse. The adrenaline replaced the fear. And when that cycle is reinforced by admiration, it becomes nearly unbreakable.

Healing came not from strength, but surrender—recognizing that the same environment that provided escape was also feeding the addiction. True recovery began when I stopped feeding the darkness and started rebuilding in the light.

Self-Help Section: Show Me Your Friends, I'll Show You Your Future

My coach used to say: "Show me your friends, I'll show you your future."
I thought it was cheesy. Something you'd find on a poster in a guidance counselor's office.

Turns out, it was a survival plan.

When I was surrounded by liars, I became one.

When I surrounded myself with addicts, I used harder.

When I walked away, I started to live.

Anthony James Hodel

Chapter 6:

The Circus Life

"They called it the circus — I called it survival."

Seventeen

I was seventeen when I started working the door. Too young to drink in the clubs I guarded, but old enough to fake authority. Cleveland after dark was its own kind of gravity—neon and noise pulling everyone who needed to feel alive for a few hours. I didn't fit in with the crowd, but belonging had never felt safe anyway.

What began as pocket money became a classroom. Every night taught me how fast people shed their masks. A joke could turn to rage in seconds. I learned to read the tension in a jawline, the twitch of a shoulder, the way silence sharpened right before a punch. That awareness kept me working—and breathing.

There was comfort in that control. Rules made sense at the door: calm people entered, chaos stayed outside. Inside my own head, no such rules existed. Maybe that's why I stayed on the edge of violence so long. If I could control the room, maybe I could control myself.

The Rush

People think bouncers go looking for fights. The truth is, fights look for you.

Sometimes it was a jealous boyfriend. Sometimes a stranger aching to bleed pride onto the pavement. The first punch always had the same soundtrack—basslines thumping, glass breaking, the crowd gasping.

Everything would slow down; my heartbeat would steady like I'd trained for it. That calm inside chaos felt like oxygen.

What hooked me wasn't just the chaos. It was the power. A rope and a clipboard turn into a crown if you let them. One nod and a night opens; one shake and it ends on the sidewalk. Inside those few square yards, I had a kind of license—unspoken but real—to step in, to use force, to make it stop. Not to start fights, but to finish them. It was the rare place where you could do violence legally if you kept it clean: clear threat, measured response, camera catching the first swing. Security tape as alibi. Incident report as absolution.

In the offseason, when football shut down and the lights at the stadium went dark, the door became my field. Friday nights were game day. Footwork at the threshold. Hips under balance. Hands inside. Leverage. I read a room the way I used to read a formation—who's leaning too far forward, who's already lost the play. The drop of a beat was the snap count. When it went bad, everything my body knew from film rooms and two-a-days clicked in. Close distance. Take angles. End it fast.

Afterward, when the noise settled and the flashing lights faded, there was always an emptiness. I'd stand there while the manager thanked me and the cops took notes, and it felt tidy—legal—like a ref's whistle had sealed the play. But tidy isn't the same as full. I'd drive home at dawn, knuckles raw, mind racing, body humming with leftover adrenaline. The city slept while I replayed every mistake I'd made that week—hand placement, timing, the one I should've seen coming sooner. Film study without the film.

I told myself it was just work, just keeping people safe. The truth was meaner: I was addicted to the feeling of being the stop sign, the last word, the one person allowed to make contact when everyone else had to flinch and watch. Nothing else gave me that kind of clarity. Not the weight room, not the quiet, not the days off. So I'd tape the cuts, wash the shirt, and be back at the door the next night. The bruises were the price of admission. The power and the permission were the fix.

Living Among Strangers

The nightlife changed faces but never its story. New clubs, new owners, same patterns—ego, envy, escape. The police knew my name; so did paramedics. We nodded in tired recognition when paths crossed at 3 a.m. Cleveland's circus had regulars, and I was one of them.

Daylight hours felt foreign. No neon, no pulse to chase. I told myself I liked the simplicity of work, but I think I liked the noise more than the paycheck. Stillness made me nervous. I didn't know how to live without a soundtrack.

Friendships stayed shallow. The job taught me that closeness was dangerous. Too many people in that world smiled to your face and sold your story later. I learned the art of surface connection—friendly, never trusting.

Walls and Patterns

Every time I'd opened up to someone, it backfired. Secrets became currency. Promises became leverage. So I built distance into my routine. Relationships followed the same script: connection, comfort, suspicion, retreat.

The first year always felt new and full of promise. By the second, I'd start watching for exits. By the third, I'd already be gone—emotionally first, physically soon after. I told myself it was mercy, sparing them from disappointment. In truth, I was sparing myself from exposure.

I became good at pretending detachment was maturity. I'd joke about being "emotionally unavailable" as if self-protection were a badge of honor. But every time I watched someone walk away, I felt that familiar echo: see, people always leave.

The problem wasn't that they left. The problem was that I kept inviting them into a story where leaving was the only ending I knew.

Loneliness in Motion

There's a special kind of isolation that comes with being surrounded by people who never really see you. Thousands of faces a week passed under those club lights; none of them knew my middle name. I lived for brief connections—five-minute conversations, shared cigarettes in alleyways, a laugh between fights.

I'd go home, peel off the sweat-stained shirt, and stare into the mirror. The eyes staring back were tired and older than they should've been. I'd wonder how the kid who used to dream about football ended up standing guard at someone else's chaos.

I told myself I didn't need anyone. The truth was simpler: I didn't know how to need anyone safely.

Toxic Cycles

Every relationship, romantic or not, eventually started to feel like déjà vu. I'd test people without telling them—ignore a call, pick an argument, create distance—just to see if they'd come closer or walk away. If they stayed, I doubted them. If they left, I felt justified. Either way, the ending was mine to control.

That pattern bled into everything—friendships, work, even faith. I could start things but never stay long enough to see them flourish.

Somewhere deep down, I believed I didn't deserve stability. Love felt temporary; loyalty felt like a myth.

Two years seemed to be the expiration date for every connection. I used to blame coincidence. Now I know it was self-sabotage disguised as protection.

Guarding the Heart

Working the door became a metaphor for how I lived.
Every night I decided who got in and who stayed out. I kept peace in public while chaos waited behind me, patient and familiar.

Sometimes, someone would slip past my defenses—a coworker who understood silence, a woman who looked past the hard exterior. But closeness triggered alarms in my chest. I'd push them away before they could see what was underneath.

It wasn't that I couldn't love. I just didn't trust love not to hurt.

Dr. Dwyer and the Chalk Talk

College didn't come until later, when exhaustion finally outweighed pride. I sat in the back of Psych 101, arms folded, scanning exits out of habit. I didn't think I belonged there either. Then Dr. Mike Dwyer started talking.

He spoke about behavior like it was language, and I realized I'd been fluent in avoidance for most of my life. "Behavior is just communication you haven't learned to translate yet," he said. That line hit harder than any punch I'd taken outside a bar.

Dwyer became, for me, what those long car rides had been when my life started to turn—a moving space where the noise thins and the direction shows up. He didn't try to fix me in a single conversation;

he gave me miles to think. His mentoring lived in the books he slid across the desk, in the lectures he stacked one clear sentence at a time, and in the chalkboard diagrams that left dust on his hands. He taught me to stop scanning exits and start reading signs.

Like a football coach, he drew X's and O's—antecedent, behavior, consequence—mapping a playbook I could actually run. When pressure spikes, run this. When the old story shows up, call an audible. Don't chase the highlight; move the chains. The board wasn't decoration; it was a route tree for my head, and running those routes started to change my thought process.

After class one day, he told me, "Anthony, your intensity is a gift, but without direction it'll destroy the container it lives in." I carried that like a game plan. I practiced—reading what he assigned, tracking my patterns, running drills when the blitz came.

I thought about that every night for weeks.

The Psychology of the Circus

In Dwyer's lectures I learned words for my chaos: trauma response, hypervigilance, avoidance, attachment. I recognized myself in every case study. Calm didn't feel peaceful—it felt suspicious. Love didn't feel safe—it felt staged.

When we studied how the body stores fear, I finally understood why my pulse spiked at kindness but steadied in conflict. I wasn't drawn to adrenaline for fun; I was chasing familiarity.

Understanding didn't fix everything, but it gave the pain a name. Naming it meant it could no longer run the show without me noticing.

Psychologist's Perspective

A psychologist would probably call it attachment trauma—the fear of closeness learned from early harm. The nervous system mistakes connection for threat, so it creates distance to feel safe.

The pattern is predictable: meet someone kind, feel exposed, invent reasons to leave. The body says run, the mind writes a script to justify it. For years, I called that independence. Now I call it fear in disguise.

Healing, I've learned, isn't inviting everyone in; it's letting one person stay and proving to yourself that safety doesn't always mean danger hiding behind it.

What I Learned in College

Psychology became my mirror. Every theory translated into confession. Cognitive Behavioral Therapy taught me that every emotion had a thought underneath it, and every thought had a memory behind it. Once I traced the chain, I could change the link.

Dr. Dwyer used to say, "Your thoughts are habits too. If you can train your body, you can retrain your mind." I'd spent years training muscles; now I started training meaning.

I began journaling at night, writing about what triggered me, how I reacted, what it reminded me of. At first the pages were angry. Over time they became quieter, more curious than defensive.

That's when growth started—not when I forgave others, but when I stopped waging war on myself.

Self-Help Section – Rebuilding Safety

1. Relearn Stillness — If calm makes you restless, stay with it anyway. Your body's not used to safety yet. Teach it slowly.
2. Build Small Trusts — Keep promises to yourself: finish tasks, show up, rest when needed. Self-trust is the foundation for trusting anyone else.
3. Let People Earn Their Way In — Time reveals truth; urgency hides it. The ones who stay through silence are the ones who belong.
4. Redefine Strength — Strength isn't about how much you can endure; it's how gently you can respond.
5. Don't Romanticize the Rush — Adrenaline feels like purpose, but it's just panic in disguise. Peace isn't boring—it's earned.
6. Find a New Tribe — Surround yourself with people who celebrate healing, not chaos. Growth is not betrayal.
7. Forgive the Guard — The version of you who built walls did it to survive. Thank him for his service, then let him rest.

The Transition

Walking away from that version of my life wasn't dramatic. There was no rock bottom, no last brawl, no flashing lights. Just quiet—the kind that felt awkward until it felt holy.

Sometimes I still feel the pull—the smell of liquor in the air, the hum of bass from a passing car, the familiar ache of wanting control. But now, instead of chasing it, I watch it fade. That's growth: not fighting the urge, but understanding why it's there.

Dr. Dwyer once said, "You don't owe your past an audience, Anthony. You owe your future some peace."

By the time I finished my degree, I wasn't trying to escape the circus anymore—I was learning how to build a life without needing the applause.

Anthony James Hodel

Chapter 7:
The Silence of Shame

"You don't talk about it. You bury it alive."

Emotional Bankruptcy

When I sat down to write this chapter, the word that came to mind was bankruptcy. Not financial bankruptcy—the kind that ruins credit—but emotional bankruptcy.

Most people hit bankruptcy after years of reckless spending, bad luck, or mounting debt. But me? I was bankrupt before I even started. Since birth, trauma had already emptied my account.ABuse, chaos, violence—it stripped me of emotional capital before I had a chance to build any.

I have fought all my life—for every inch, every opportunity, every ounce of peace. That fight still continues today. So when I hear the phrase "white privilege," it hits me like a slap in the face. What privilege? Was I privileged when I was being violated as a child? Was I privileged while I was fighting to survive in a world that tried to erase me before I could even find myself?

People make assumptions because they don't know what they don't know—and that kind of blindness is the purest form of ignorance. There's an old saying: assumptions make assholes out of all of us. I've lived that truth. Too many judge the outcome without ever asking about the cost.

I carried shame like a crushing debt. And like any debtor drowning in bills, I tried to hide it, cover it, make the minimum payments of silence. I convinced myself if I didn't talk about it, nobody would notice. That silence became my prison.

The Male Code of Silence

Men don't talk. That's the script we're handed. "Be tough. Shake it off. Move on." To admit pain is to admit weakness. And weakness gets exploited.

So we bury it. We stay silent out of compliance, fear, or shame. But silence has a price—it corrodes from within. I'm convinced more men than anyone realizes are living with scars of abuse—sexual, physical, emotional. But they keep it hidden because the world doesn't expect men to be victims. Research backs this: boys and men are less likely than girls and women to disclose sexual abuse, and when they do, they often disclose later in life—a double burden of trauma and silence.

When women speak of abuse, society leans in with sympathy, even if judgment follows. When men speak of it, we're met with confusion, disbelief, or worse—mockery. That stigma builds the walls of our prison. And it distorts the numbers we *do* see, because under-reporting by males is real. Even so, the data that *are* available are sobering.

In the U.S., across a lifetime:

- **Sexual violence (contact):** Over half of women and almost **1 in 3 men** report sexual violence involving physical contact. **Rape (completed or attempted)** touches about **1 in 4 women** and **~1 in 26 men**. For men, another form that isn't always called "rape" in surveys—**being made to penetrate**—is reported by **about 1 in 9**. These are not edge cases; they're millions of lives.

- **Intimate partner violence (IPV):** About **41% of U.S. women** and **26% of U.S. men** have experienced **contact sexual violence, physical violence, or stalking by a partner** and reported related impacts. Psychological aggression alone has touched **~61 million women and ~53 million men**. And for many men who experience severe sexual victimization, **the first incident happens before 25**.

For teens (high school, U.S. 2021): the gap is stark but not one-sided.

- **Lifetime forced sex: 13.5% of girls** vs **3.6% of boys**.
- **Past-year sexual violence by *anyone*: 17.9% of girls** vs **4.6% of boys**.
- **Past-year sexual dating violence: 15.3% of girls** vs **4.0% of boys**.
  Girls face higher measured rates, but note that teen boys *do* report these harms—and male under-disclosure is well documented.

Childhood, outside the U.S. (to show the pattern holds): In England and Wales (2025), nearly **3 in 10 adults** say they were abused as children (**31.5% of women, 26.4% of men**). **Sexual abuse** shows the largest sex gap (**13.9% of women vs 4.1% of men**), while **physical abuse** showed **no significant sex difference**—reminding us that boys are not spared physical or emotional harm.

Globally (children): A 2025 JAMA Pediatrics meta-analysis found **6.1% of children reported completed forced sexual intercourse** in their lifetime—**6.8% of girls** and **3.3% of boys**—with broader contact sexual violence even higher. These figures likely *underestimate* reality, especially for boys.

Older adults (60+): Abuse doesn't fade with age. Worldwide, about **1 in 6** older people experience some form of abuse in community settings in a given year; rates in institutions are higher, and sex-specific patterns vary by type and study. The takeaway is simple: **older men and women are both at risk**, and many never report.

When you add it up, the stereotype that "men aren't victims" collapses. Men *are* victims—of sexual assault, of physical harm, of emotional and psychological abuse. The difference is that our culture often tells us to minimize it, forget it, or drink it away. And that has a cost measured in broken families, buried addictions, and lives that never quite come back online.

This is another important prong to this entire book—the main reason I penned it. As men, we need to seek help. We need to move on and grow. We can't be effective fathers, leaders, or even decent men until we face our trauma head-on. I know this to be one hundred percent true.

That's why I decided to speak out. The team is bigger than me—again. If I can help guide even one person away from pain, from drugs, from addiction, then this was all worth it. What started as a therapist's assignment has become a driving force in my life—a mission to turn my pain into purpose and my silence into service.

If you (or a reader) need a first step: the **RAINN National Sexual Assault Hotline (800-656-HOPE)** offers confidential support 24/7 in the U.S.; similar services exist internationally. Reaching out isn't weakness—it's the beginning of repair.

Violence as a Language

I didn't cry about it. I didn't talk about it. Instead, I fought. Silence turned into violence. My trauma was a volcano that never erupted in words, only in fists.

Violence started so young in me—it built its residency in my body, soul, and mind. For years, I thought it was just who I was. But if you have a child who's fighting, lashing out, or always angry, it's not random—it's a response. It's trauma showing itself because it can't speak any other language. Violence is the reaction to the actions that broke them. Prove me wrong.

Most of the time I walked around looking normal, but in reality, I was a ticking time bomb. The fuse was alcohol. Mix booze with a bad mood and someone poking the bear, and suddenly all the buried rage erupted.

Violence was my minimum payment on the debt of silence. I thought I was buying myself relief, but the bill always came back bigger.

The Addict in Disguise

People point fingers at crackheads, meth heads, drunks. They label addiction as dirty, weak, shameful. But addiction wears many faces. Mine was steroids, rage, silence—and sex.

I dodged using other drugs because, as a teenager, I already told myself: no more rabbit holes, no more demons. I couldn't handle any more. Some people don't have that ability to say when. They're zero to a hundred, real quick. I had a brake pedal—faulty and low on pads—but I could still come to a slow, grinding stop. That ability to self-reflect, to see the cliff before I went over it, saved my life without question.

The truth is, addiction is just escape. Some escape in bottles, some in needles, some in sex, some in violence. I escaped by building walls of muscle and pretending nothing touched me. But the shame was always there, buried alive, collecting penalties.

The Dead Eyes

After my father died, I went through his house and found a box of old childhood photos. I stopped at one picture in particular—me as a boy, during the peak of my trauma. What hit me hardest wasn't the setting or the clothes. It was my eyes.

They were dead. No spark. No joy. Just emptiness.

When my father lay in his hospice bed, his eyes looked the same—gray, hollow, lifeless. I saw that same look in my own reflection so many times that it terrified me. That same dull gray haunted me because I knew what it meant: he was gone, and I wasn't far from that feeling myself. I tried to close his eyes before they took him, but I couldn't. They stayed half open, staring through me.

You've probably heard the phrase "their eyes are smiling." Makes sense, doesn't it? Because when the soul is alive, you see it in the eyes. And when it's gone—you see that too.

And I realized I'd seen those same eyes in my reflection during some of my darkest adult years—during my divorce, during the collapse of my company, and even in magazine articles where I was being celebrated for my "success." The world thought I was on top of everything, but my eyes told the truth.

That's what emotional bankruptcy looks like—empty eyes staring back, even when the world sees a full bank account.

Masks of Success

Awards. Cars. Houses. Rolexes. All of it was window dressing for a man rotting inside. People shook my hand and envied my achievements, but they didn't see the dead eyes staring back in the photos. They didn't know that success doesn't silence shame—it amplifies it.

As I spent my mid-twenties with chest pains and random episodes of tears, everyone around me thought my life was perfect. I was the walking dead. I couldn't decode the root of my pain; I just knew I wasn't living—I was performing. I was living a lie, trapped in a body that looked successful but carried a soul that was collapsing.

Because when you reach the top and still feel empty, that's when you realize the problem isn't the world. It's you.

The Mirror Talk

After three years of deep depression, drowning in failure, bad headlines, and silence, I looked in the mirror one morning and finally said out loud: "You gotta snap out of this."

It was—even to this day—the toughest period of my life. I lived in Tremont, in an upscale condo, chased pretty girls, and hid my lies. There were mornings I'd wake up in actual physical pain. The stress of the courts, the business pressure, and the personal chaos took their toll on my body. Every day started the same way: staring into the mirror, giving myself a pep talk like I was gearing up for a game. I thought I was losing my mind, but the truth is, I was finally starting to find it. What I thought was insanity was actually the beginning of sanity—the moment I stopped running from myself.

For the first time, I confronted myself—not the mask, not the businessman, not the athlete. Just the broken kid who grew into a broken man. And I realized something profound: silence hadn't protected me—it had poisoned me.

That was my personal declaration of bankruptcy—the point where I admitted the truth, wiped away the denial, and started over.

Breaking the Silence

The first step to healing isn't forgiveness. It isn't therapy. It isn't revenge. It's acknowledgment. It's saying the words out loud: Yes, this happened to me.

And once you say it—once you stop burying it—you take away its power. That's when you begin sorting it out internally, privately. Before you go public, you wrestle with the ghosts in your own heart. That's where healing begins. That's when you stop paying interest on someone else's crimes.

Psychologists say that silence is one of the most damaging coping mechanisms a trauma survivor can adopt. According to research from the American Psychological Association, repressed trauma doesn't disappear—it embeds itself in the nervous system. The body stores the story the mind refuses to tell. That's why so many trauma survivors experience physical symptoms: anxiety, chest pain, insomnia, digestive issues, migraines, and muscle tension. You don't just "remember" trauma—you relive it, every day.

Dr. Bessel van der Kolk, author of The Body Keeps the Score, explains that healing requires transforming traumatic memory into narrative memory—putting pain into words so the brain can reprocess it. Until then, it stays trapped in the emotional centers of the brain like a loop, constantly replaying. That's why speaking out—whether to a therapist, a friend, or even a journal—isn't just emotional; it's neurological. You're literally rewiring the brain to separate the event from your identity.

That's also why men struggle more with unresolved trauma. Studies show that men are four times less likely than women to seek therapy. Cultural conditioning teaches us that vulnerability is weakness, but modern neuroscience proves the opposite.

Vulnerability is regulation—it reduces cortisol, lowers heart rate, and re-engages the logical prefrontal cortex, which trauma shuts down.

When you speak, you heal. When you suppress, you stay sick.

It's not about dramatizing your pain—it's about integrating it. Trauma is like a broken bone that never set properly. You can keep walking on it, but it'll always hurt until you realign it. Speaking out, therapy, journaling, meditation—all of these are ways of re-setting the bone of your soul so it can finally heal straight.

The hardest part of breaking silence is facing what comes next—the emotions, the flashbacks, the guilt, the disbelief. But psychologists agree: what feels like breaking down is actually breaking through. It's your nervous system releasing what it's carried for years.

You can't heal what you won't face. And you can't face what you refuse to name. Speaking is naming. Naming is freeing.

Speaking for the Silenced

Men need to know this: you are not alone. You're not weak for admitting what happened. In fact, your strength lies in your honesty. Somebody out there is waiting for you to speak so they can finally feel safe enough to speak too. That's the chain reaction of healing.

Don't be ashamed. Be empowered in your pain. File emotional bankruptcy if you need to. Because sometimes clearing the books is the only way to build wealth again.

This is my driving force. This is my why. My father left me well off financially, but more importantly, he left me with the opportunity to create a legacy. When I told him—at thirty-two years old—what I had endured with my brother, how horrific it was, and that I feared it might have continued inside his own home, he didn't know what to say. He went silent.

But silence wasn't new to our family—it was generational. The difference is, I broke the chain. I'm strong now. Strong enough to be the voice my father couldn't be, the protector he didn't know how to become.

Even in death, he still speaks to me. His ashes sit in an urn on my bookshelf, and every day that old watch of his—still ticking and beeping—reminds me that time keeps moving, that growth never stops. It's his way of saying, keep going, son.

God willing, this book will generate the conversations men have avoided for generations. It will create connections rooted in truth and healing. And maybe, just maybe, when others find the courage to speak, it will close the book of trauma I've been carrying my whole life.

Because my father may not have found his words in life, but through me—and through these pages—he's finally speaking.

A Psychologist's Perspective

From a clinical standpoint, this chapter is a living case study of how early trauma reshapes the brain, body, and sense of identity. The behaviors I described—rage, addiction, silence, overachievement—aren't random; they're neurological adaptations.

Psychologists explain that when a child grows up in chaos or abuse, the brain's alarm system (the amygdala) stays stuck in survival mode. The logical, decision-making part of the brain (the prefrontal cortex) goes offline, replaced by fight, flight, or freeze. Years later, that same wiring triggers panic, anger, or emotional shutdown during stress.

In men especially, cultural conditioning compounds this. Society trains us to replace vulnerability with aggression, to equate emotion with weakness. Over time, the nervous system becomes addicted to adrenaline and numb to peace. That's why many trauma survivors, particularly men, seek stimulation—through work, sex, risk, or violence—to feel anything at all.

Therapeutically, the path forward isn't to erase those impulses but to understand them. Healing begins when awareness replaces shame. When we label the response for what it is—a survival pattern—we reclaim control. Psychologists emphasize integrating the emotional and rational brains through consistent practices: talk therapy, mindfulness, EMDR, breathwork, journaling. These help re-wire the stress circuits and allow the body to feel safe again.

In short, silence is the symptom; expression is the treatment. The goal is not to forget the past but to metabolize it—to turn raw pain into organized memory, and memory into wisdom.

The Road Out of Bankruptcy – Self-Help Lessons

Silence nearly bankrupted my soul. Shame collected interest until I was walking around with nothing left. But just like financial bankruptcy isn't the end of your life, emotional bankruptcy doesn't mean you're finished either. It means you get to start over.

Here are the steps that carried me forward—and can carry you too:

1. **Face the Ledger Honestly**

   Stop pretending your books balance. Write down what happened. Admit the numbers don't add up. Naming it is the first deposit back into your account.

2. **Stop Paying Interest on Other People's Crimes**

The abuse wasn't your fault. The trauma wasn't your choice. But silence makes you pay for it over and over again. The day you speak is the day you cancel that debt.

3. **Build Emotional Credit Slowly**

   Healing isn't a lottery win. It's small deposits: keeping one promise to yourself, telling one safe person the truth, setting one boundary. That's how you rebuild.

4. **Surround Yourself with Wealthy People (Emotionally)**

   Show me your friends, I'll show you your future. Stay close to people who invest in you, who tell the truth, who hold space for you. They'll add compound interest to your growth.

5. **Invest in Healing Like Your Life Depends on It—Because It Does**

   Therapy, journaling, faith, exercise—whatever your method is, treat it as oxygen. Material things won't fill the hole. Peace will.

6. **Remember: Bankruptcy Is Not the End, It's the Beginning**

   Declaring bankruptcy doesn't make you weak; it makes you free. You wipe the slate and rebuild on honesty instead of illusion.

The Rearview Mirror

The abuse happened. The shame happened. The silence happened. You can't change it. You can't replay it. The game is already in the books.

But like in football, you don't win by staring at the last play. You win by focusing on the next down. How you prepare, how you recover, how you grow—that's redemption.

We're never perfect. But you don't need perfection to rise. You just need the courage to take your perfect mess and build something out of it.

So stop burying it alive. Say it. Face it. Own it. Then walk out of the silence. Declare bankruptcy if you have to—and then rebuild from scratch.

Anthony James Hodel

Chapter 8:
The Mirror Doesn't Lie

"You can fool the world, but the mirror keeps score."

Every wild night has a morning after. The lights turn off, the music dies down, the bodies leave, and you're left with silence. That silence used to terrify me.

I'd wake up hungover, staring into a bathroom mirror that refused to negotiate with my lies. My reflection didn't care about the excuses I gave everyone else: I'm just blowing off steam, or I deserve this after everything I've been through.

The truth stared back with bloodshot eyes. The truth was ugly.

Trauma and addiction don't just eat away at you—they devour everyone close to you. My addictions didn't just cost me money, muscle, or opportunities. They cost me a marriage. They cost me time I'll never get back with my kids.

Love doesn't survive when addiction calls the plays. I would trade stability for the thrill of something new, someone new. It wasn't about love or intimacy—it was about escape. The high of wondering how a new person would make me feel was stronger than the anchor of staying grounded. Every "yes" to that question was a "no" to my family.

In my first marriage, I was ignored. Intimacy was dull, almost nonexistent, and the emotional disconnect became suffocating. I felt like I was living beside someone, not with them. And instead of confronting it, I went off the rails. I had affairs on top of affairs, trying to keep my head above water emotionally—trying to feel something.

One day, out of frustration, I told her I was starving for connection, for passion, for life. Her response wasn't love or effort—it was indifference. She looked me dead in the eye and said, "Then get a girlfriend."

So, I did. About a dozen of them.

Each one was stronger, more confident, more alive. It felt like an upgrade in every way. But what I didn't realize then was that I wasn't chasing women—I was chasing dopamine. The buzz, the rush, the chemical hit that made me forget how empty I really was.

Desk. Conference rooms. Parking lots. Six-thirty in the morning—it didn't matter. I was high on the chase, drunk on lust, feeding an addiction that had nothing to do with sex and everything to do with control, validation, and escape.

At that moment, I thought I was winning. In reality, I was losing everything that actually mattered.

The irony was brutal. I told myself I didn't like strip clubs, didn't like that kind of world—but I had the mold of it living with me. It was transactional, cold, performative. I knew I was being used, and I still stayed in it. What was I thinking?

That's the insanity of addiction—it convinces you that pain is passion, that chaos is connection, and that the next person will somehow fill the emptiness the last one couldn't.

Here's what burned me the most: even if I had been perfect, I still couldn't have made some people happy. They had their own demons.

Their own traumas. Their own addictions—shopping, money, manipulation.

I couldn't fix them, and I couldn't unwind what they did. I watched money disappear. I saw my kids withheld and used as bargaining chips for more child support. I lived through manipulation that made me question my own sanity.

But this isn't about pointing fingers at their flaws or lack of character. This is about me owning mine.

Addiction doesn't always look like a bottle or a needle. Mine wore high heels, perfume, and carried the rush of a new encounter. My sex addiction was the sickness that destroyed everything stable in my life.

For several years, I spent upwards of seven to ten thousand dollars a month feeding that demon. Exotic women from all over the world flew in to meet men like me—men willing to fund their lifestyle in exchange for the illusion of connection. These weren't drug addicts or desperate hustlers; these were professionals who made huge money by knowing exactly how to feed my emptiness.

I justified it: I can afford it. I'm not hurting anyone. But the truth was I was bleeding out—financially, emotionally, spiritually. Money can't fill the hole left by trauma; it only digs it deeper.

Drinking wasn't an everyday thing for me, but when it came, it came hard and ugly. Dirty martinis that led to fights. Vodka doubles on the rocks with lime that ended with handcuffs. A couple bottles of wine in one night that unlocked rage I thought I'd buried. Any time I had legal problems outside of child-support wars, alcohol was in the room. Every arrest. Every night I woke up in a cell or covered in blood—it was always booze that lit the fuse.

My anger was already a live wire. Alcohol just poured gasoline on it.

Why Some Survivors of Abuse Cheat: a "Mask" Chasing the Same Highs—and Keeping People Out

Not everyone who survives abuse cheats. And cheating is never "justified."

But for some survivors, infidelity can function like a *mask*—what you called a "mas"—that chases familiar highs while keeping true intimacy at arm's length.

The quick idea

Abuse wires the nervous system to expect intensity, unpredictability, and danger. In that state, calm closeness can feel foreign—even unsafe. Cheating can deliver short bursts of validation, thrill, and control (the "highs"), while secretly preventing a partner from ever getting all the way in (the "mask").

How the "high" gets hooked to the heart

- **Survival chemistry.** Long-term stress trains the body to run on adrenaline and cortisol. Risk, novelty, and secrecy can dump dopamine into that system. The hit isn't about pleasure alone; it's about *regulation*—feeling relief from a background hum of fear or numbness.

- **Limerence as painkiller.** Early-stage infatuation can mute shame, quiet intrusive memories, and create a powerful sense of being special. When life has taught you you're disposable, that feeling becomes intoxicating.

- **Familiar chaos.** If chaos was the baseline in past relationships or childhood, your body might equate calm with danger and turbulence with "home." Reaching for the same highs is a way to re-create a known rhythm, even if it hurts.

How cheating functions as a mask

1. **Distance without breaking up.** "If I'm not fully in, you can't fully hurt me." Infidelity keeps a secret barrier that dilutes vulnerability.

2. **Control after powerlessness.** When someone once took your choices away, a hidden life can feel like reclaiming choice—*I decide what happens to me now*—even as it violates your partner's consent.

3. **Validation on tap.** External attention can anesthetize old beliefs like "I'm unlovable." The relief is real but rented; it vanishes when the interaction ends, so the chase resumes.

4. **Repetition of the template.** We repeat what we learned until we heal it. If love once came with fear, betrayal, or walking on eggshells, the body may unconsciously cue behaviors that recreate that pairing.

5. **Pre-emptive self-sabotage.** "You'll leave me anyway, so I'll make it happen on my terms." Destroying closeness before closeness can reject you is a warped form of self-protection.

6. **Compartmentalization and numbness.** Dissociation—splitting off thoughts, feelings, or identity pieces—can make double lives *feel* separate, reducing guilt in the moment but multiplying harm later.

Why it *doesn't* let anyone in

- **Intimacy = exposure.** Being truly seen threatens the defenses that kept you safe. Secrets keep you in charge of how much you're known.

- **Closeness triggers alarms.** Safety can feel suspicious when danger was normal. Pushing a partner away with betrayal keeps the "alarm quiet" by preventing the depth that awakens old terror.

- **Testing love through harm.** "Will you still want me if I prove I'm unworthy?" It's a test no relationship can pass without breaking.

Understanding without excusing

Two truths can sit together:

- **Trauma explains behavior.** These patterns are understandable survival strategies.

- **You're still responsible.** Healing means owning the impact, ending the behavior, and rebuilding (or releasing) the relationship with integrity.

If this is you: practical ways to change the pattern

- **Name the urge for what it is.** Not a sign you "picked the wrong partner," but a *regulation strategy* your body trusts. Say: *My nervous system wants relief; cheating is the old route.*

- **Build tolerance for safety.** Practice tiny "micro-doses" of calm: 30–60 seconds of slow breathing, orienting to the room, feeling feet on the ground. Learn that steady isn't dangerous; it's different.

- **Make a rupture plan.** Before urges hit:

    o   15-minute delay rule (no acting for 15 minutes; reset timer as needed).

    o   One person you can text, "I'm in the spiral; help me ride it out."

    o   One body-based reset (walk, cold water on wrists, step outside).

- **Close the portals.** Delete secret accounts and risky contacts. Create friction where you used to find ease.

- **Radical clarity about agreements.** If monogamy feels suffocating, don't cheat—*say so*. Explore ethical structures (or decide this relationship isn't a fit) with transparency and consent.

- **Seek trauma-informed help.** Modalities like EMDR, somatic therapies, and trauma-focused CBT can help your body learn safety while your mind learns new choices.

- **Tell the whole truth once.** If you're repairing, avoid "trickle truth." Own the behavior, its impact, and your plan for change. Offer transparency appropriate to what your partner needs for healing.

- **Track wins, not just slips.** Keep a log of triggers, urges, and how you rode them out. Teach your brain that new routes *work*.

If you're the partner who was betrayed

- **It wasn't your job to prevent this.** Their trauma context can explain *why*—it does not blame *you*.

- **Set and enforce boundaries.** Access to devices, therapy requirements, living arrangements—define the conditions under which you'll consider rebuilding.

- **Protect your nervous system.** Individual support matters. You don't have to decide quickly whether to stay or go.

- **You're allowed to leave.** Compassion for someone's trauma and clarity about your limits can coexist.

Reflection prompts (for the person who cheated)

- When do I feel most compelled to seek the "high"? What happened in the 24 hours before the urge?

- What sensations (tight chest, buzzing, numbness) tell me I'm dysregulated?

- If cheating is a mask, what parts of me does it hide? What would letting someone in *actually* require?

- What would it look like to pursue intensity *inside* the relationship—adventure, novelty, play—without betrayal?

Bottom line

For some survivors of abuse, cheating isn't about a lack of love; it's about a nervous system still living in yesterday. The affair becomes a *mask*—a way to chase familiar highs and avoid being seen. You didn't choose the abuse. You *do* choose what you do now. Healing is possible, and it starts with telling the truth, learning safe ways to regulate, and letting someone in—first yourself, then the person you love.

The Jail Cell

One night still sticks like a shard in my memory. A downtown bar, neon lights, laughter too loud to be real. I'd promised myself just one drink. That turned into three dirty martinis, a vodka double, and then another.

Some guy bumped into me—no big deal—but my ego was already drunk. I shoved him. He shoved back. Chairs crashed. Glass shattered. I don't remember the exact punch that dropped him, only the sirens after.

Next thing I knew, I was sitting on a cold concrete bench, wrists aching from the cuffs. My head pounded. My shirt was soaked with someone's blood—maybe his, maybe mine. The officer looked at me and said, "You again?"

That hit harder than the punch. *You again.*

When the adrenaline drained, shame took its place. The hangover wasn't just physical—it was spiritual. I remember staring at that scratched stainless-steel mirror in the holding cell and thinking, *this is who you've become.* The muscle, the bravado, the money—it's all bullshit. You're just another angry drunk with regrets waiting for morning release.

And if that wasn't enough chaos, my personal life was detonating too. My first wife was spending a thousand dollars a day—luxury, designer everything, no limits—and when it all started collapsing, she left me with a $750,000 shareholder loan on the books. Then she called the feds on me.

Sounds crazy, right? She was—and still is—something special, if you know what I mean.

At that moment, sitting in that cell, I realized it wasn't just bad luck or bad company—it was me. I had chosen every bit of the madness I was drowning in.

We all cope differently. Some people run to a bottle. Some to a needle. Some to shopping sprees. I learned firsthand that "retail therapy" isn't cute—it's a sickness. The spending, the stealing, the endless need for more—it's just another way to cover wounds.

When I walked away from relationships, I thought I was leaving chaos behind. But chaos has a way of following you, especially when children and money are involved.

The turning point came in counseling. Sitting in that chair—no more excuses, no more football, no more high-end hookers to distract me. Just me, my rage, and the truth.

I had to face anger head-on. For years, anger had been my armor. Drinking was my shield. Violence was my outlet. Cheating was my escape. Strip all that away, and what was left? A broken man in his fifties staring at himself in the mirror. And for the first time, I didn't look away.

The Psychology of the Mirror (The Looking-Glass Self)

In counseling, I learned something that hit me harder than any punch I'd ever thrown or taken—something psychologists call the Looking-Glass Self.

It's the idea that we build our sense of who we are by seeing ourselves reflected through the eyes of others. From childhood, we start forming our identity based on how we think people perceive us. Approval feels like oxygen. Rejection feels like death.

For most of my life, my "mirror" wasn't made of glass—it was made of other people's opinions. Coaches, women, business partners, even strangers on social media—they all became my reflection. If they thought I was powerful, I felt powerful. If they thought I was broken, I tried harder to prove them wrong.

But that's the danger of the Looking-Glass Self: when your reflection is in someone else's hands, you'll never really know who you are. You just keep shape-shifting, performing, pleasing—until the mirror shatters and you don't recognize your own face anymore.

Counseling forced me to build a new mirror, one made of truth instead of validation. It wasn't easy. For the first time, I had to look at the man behind the mask—without the applause, without the women, without the distraction. Just me.

And the hardest part? Learning to accept that the reflection I see now—flawed, scarred, and imperfect—is finally real.

Lessons in the Mirror

1. You can't fix everyone. No matter how hard you try, you can't heal someone else's trauma. That's their work.
2. Addiction is a thief. It steals your time, your relationships, and your peace—and it always takes more than it gives.
3. Anger plus alcohol equals prison. Every legal problem outside of child support traced back to booze. Know your triggers before they ruin you.
4. Counseling isn't weakness. It's war against the lies you've believed for too long.

5. Forgiveness is for you. I had to forgive myself before I could move forward. Carrying shame and regret was just another chain.

A Psychologist's Perspective

From a psychologist's standpoint, Chapter 8 reflects a textbook pattern of trauma-driven addiction and self-regulation failure. What you experienced—the constant chasing of dopamine, the reckless need for validation, and the emotional detachment from intimacy—aligns with what clinicians describe as a trauma loop.

When early pain and rejection go unresolved, the brain seeks temporary relief through stimulation. Whether it's sex, alcohol, spending, or power, each rush floods the system with dopamine and momentarily overrides the body's stress chemistry. But once the high fades, the emptiness returns—usually deeper than before. That's why relapse feels almost magnetic. The brain remembers the pleasure but forgets the pain until it hits again.

This story also captures the phenomenon of displaced control. Many trauma survivors unconsciously trade emotional vulnerability for dominance or performance—sex, business, or even violence—because those areas provide predictable outcomes. Vulnerability, by contrast, feels unsafe. The person learns to equate intimacy with danger and control with survival.

The Looking-Glass Self adds another layer of complexity. Psychologically, when someone builds identity around external validation, the loss of admiration or attention triggers an existential collapse. I wasn't just losing relationships—I was losing reflections of myself. The result is a cycle of chasing new mirrors to feel momentarily whole again.

From a therapeutic lens, my breakthrough in counseling—facing my reflection without distraction—marks the beginning of what psychologists call self-integration. It's when fragmented identities (the addict, the husband, the fighter, the provider) start merging into one authentic self. The process is brutal, but it's the only road to peace.

Self-Help: Facing Your Own Mirror

- Stop outsourcing blame. Write down every excuse you've been telling yourself, then cross them out one by one. The reflection in the mirror is the only one responsible.
- Audit your addictions. Be honest: what do you run to when life feels heavy—sex, shopping, drinking? Name it. You can't fight what you won't face.
- Count the true cost. Put a dollar figure, an hour count, or a memory tally on your addiction. When I added mine up, it was millions of dollars and years I'll never get back.
- Know your booze truth. If alcohol turns you into someone you don't recognize, own it. That "once in a while" night can ruin your life.
- Choose healing over thrills. Thrills fade. Healing compounds. It's boring, it's slow, but it's the only way to peace.
- Get help. Counseling, recovery groups, mentors—whatever it takes. Don't let pride keep you chained.
- Accept the losses. You can't get back the years, the money, or the moments. But you can stop bleeding out more of them today.

I'm not writing this from the seat of judgment. I'm writing it from the seat of survival. My trauma and addictions cost me marriage, kids' memories, and years I'll never get back.

For years, I thought money, women, and alcohol were medicine. They weren't. They were poison dressed up as pleasure.

But the mirror doesn't lie. And the day I finally stared at it—without booze, without rage, without another body in my bed—was the day I started becoming a man I could live with.

Not perfect. Not polished. But finally, real.

Chapter 9:

Facing Ghosts

"Every step forward felt like a climb out of the pit I dug myself."

The Pit

Rock bottom wasn't a place. It was a condition.

It was the hollow echo of silence in a house where laughter used to live. It was staring at court papers that read more like a bill of sale for your freedom than legal documents. It was waking up hungover, the taste of vodka still on your tongue, with bruises on your knuckles and no memory of what you'd swung at.

For me, the pit looked like a man who had burned through fortunes, wrecked relationships, and turned every "new start" into another demolition project. I had women, I had booze, I had money—but I didn't have me.

And truthfully, I was like the Cleveland Browns—I always found creative and amazing ways to fuck up. I didn't just fall once; I fell over and over, inventing new ways to sabotage my own progress. Just when I thought I had hit rock bottom, I'd find a new level beneath it. I didn't have one pit; I had several—my life looked like a golf course full of traps, each one waiting for me to land in it.

One pit still burns in my memory: I had promised my mother and father-in-law that I would take care of their daughter. I meant it. I looked them in the eye and gave my word. But I failed—spectacularly—during our dual alcohol-fueled fights. That's why today I don't drink. It's not about being sober for a program or a rulebook—it's because I'm genuinely afraid of what still lives deep inside me.

When I'm sober, I never raise my voice. I never even speak out of tone with her. But under the influence, I became a version of myself that I despised.

Her dad had spoken to me before the wedding, worried about her well-being because of her past relationships. I told him, man-to-man, that she'd be safe with me—that I'd protect her, respect her, and love her. And then I broke that promise.

He lived down in Alabama, and I loved our talks. We'd sit outside, smoke cigars, and talk about life. It felt like the father figure I had been searching for—even as a grown man. I always wanted to apologize to him. I planned to go there, face him, and own my mistakes. I figured he had his demons too, but I wanted to show him that I recognized mine and that he didn't have to worry about his daughter anymore.

I never got the chance. He passed before I could make things right. That haunts me to this day.

The pit is deep not because you fall, but because you dig. Every lie I told myself was another shovelful of dirt. "I'll quit tomorrow." Dig. "I deserve this night out." Dig. "It's not my fault." Dig. Before long, the ladder out looked like it was miles above my head.

The First Step

Nobody tells you that climbing out of the pit doesn't start with a heroic leap. It starts with the smallest, dumbest little step.

For me, it wasn't some glorious Hollywood moment. No violins, no spotlight. It was deciding not to pour a drink that night. It was walking away when a fight was inches away.

It was hard. Stupidly hard. I was used to living on the high of chaos—booze, women, fights, adrenaline. Saying no felt like dying. But one day became two. Two became a week. Then I stumbled, fell back down a few stairs, but I knew now there were stairs. That mattered.

When I first came home from jail, everything felt brand new. The air smelled fresher. The sun looked brighter. I had that typical "I'm free, I'm changed, I'm never going back" kind of attitude. I walked out with hope in my chest, thinking I'd left the old me behind those bars.

I know that if I hadn't gone to jail, I would have kept burying everything and lived a toxic life all the way to my death. Jail felt like God's way of stopping me—forcing me to confront the deep trauma I'd spent years hiding. On those cold nights it was just me and my thoughts. I'd pull a sheet over my whole body to block the sight of the brick walls, the cold steel bunk, the fact that I was caged. Under that cover, the past found me anyway. The memories of my childhood abuse were so vivid I could taste them, smell them. I cried, and for once I didn't run. I finally admitted: this is why I'm here—to stop everything, to face what happened, to feel it and tell the truth, and to begin the work of healing instead of letting the pain keep steering my life.

But a few years later, I realized freedom wasn't about walking out of a cell—it was about facing the one you still carried inside. The little devil didn't disappear; he just waited. And slowly, when life got hard again, I found myself fighting him daily.

Things got rough. Bills, relationships, expectations—all of it piled up. I had to face uncomfortable truths about myself and my situation. I had to admit that "changed" wasn't a permanent state—it was a daily choice.

What I learned this time around is that none of this is a sprint. It's more like a Forrest Gump kind of run—long, lonely, and unpredictable. You just keep moving, one mile at a time, through storms, sunshine, and pain. Recovery isn't fireworks. It's a slow burn, a marathon of discipline, humility, and self-awareness.

Psychologists say recovery isn't a short-term event; it's a long-term process of rewiring the brain. The habits, the chemicals, the emotional triggers—they don't vanish overnight. The neural pathways that once fed your addiction still exist, waiting for a spark. Studies show that true behavioral recovery takes years of consistent change, not weeks of good intentions. It's like building new muscle memory for your mind.

That's why I stopped chasing perfection and started chasing consistency. Because no one wins this battle in a weekend. You win it inch by inch, breath by breath, choosing the right thing over the easy thing—every single day.

Reps Build Strength

In the gym, nobody gets jacked on day one. You push, you sweat, you tear the muscle fibers. Then they rebuild. Over and over. That's what redemption felt like.

Every time I said no to the old life, I tore a fiber of who I used to be. And every time I chose discipline instead of chaos, I rebuilt a stronger version of myself.

I took the same obsessive drive that once fueled steroids, escort sites, Backpage ads, and Craigslist hookups, and redirected it. Business became my new addiction. Building something—whether it was an auto shop, a marketing company, or just a vision for the future—gave me the same thrill, but without the hangover, without the cops, without the shame.

Redemption is repetition. Not fireworks.

The reps have gotten easier over time—but not because life got lighter. They got easier because I learned to reduce the weight. For years, I tried to fix everything at once—every trauma, every addiction, every mistake. I wanted to bench-press my entire past. That never works.

What I've learned is that healing, like fitness, is progressive. You don't fix decades of damage overnight. It took years of abuse to build the rock; it will take years to chip away at it. You can't sprint through recovery. You have to pace yourself, set one goal, and master it before moving to the next.

Psychologists say people fall hard and fast in addiction because of the same neural systems that drive survival. The brain's reward circuits—mainly dopamine—get hijacked. The hit, the rush, the escape—it all mimics purpose and comfort. Your brain doesn't know it's killing you; it just knows it wants that feeling again. That's why addicts relapse so quickly—it's biology waging war against logic.

So I stopped trying to outmuscle the addiction and started outsmarting it. One day, one rep, one choice at a time.

Facing the Ghosts

The demons didn't vanish. They never do. They sit in the corner, whispering:

"Remember how good she felt?"
"One drink won't kill you."
"Anger makes you powerful."

There were nights when I almost believed them. Nights when my phone lit up with numbers that could've put me right back into a thousand-dollar weekend of self-destruction. Nights when the craving for control or the rush of forbidden sex almost won.

But here's the truth: temptation doesn't go away—you outgrow it. The same way a kid outgrows toys, you outgrow demons by refusing to play their games.

One story sticks: I was a few months into my climb out when I found myself standing outside a sex club, my hand on the door. For a split second, I could already feel the heat of the room and the chaos waiting inside. But I didn't go in. I walked to my car, sat in silence, and cried like a kid. Not because I was weak—but because, for once, I had chosen differently. That was strength.

Psychologists say those "ghosts" that reappear from the past aren't random—they're neurological echoes. When we experience trauma or repeat destructive behavior, the brain builds emotional memory circuits that don't fade easily. They stay dormant, waiting for familiar triggers—stress, loneliness, anger—to reactivate them.

That's why you can be years sober, miles away from the chaos, and suddenly feel the old urges like they never left. The brain replays what it once believed was survival. Those ghosts are unfinished emotional files—memories the mind keeps reopening, begging you to finally process what you ran from.

Facing the ghosts isn't about erasing them; it's about understanding them. When you stop fearing the reappearance of your past and instead learn from it, you begin to reclaim control.

I still see mine sometimes—in quiet moments, in certain songs, in familiar scents. But now I don't run. I nod, acknowledge them, and remind myself: "You don't own me anymore."

Forgiveness

Forgiveness was, by far, the hardest step. Not forgiving others—I was part of it. I was in the ring. I threw punches, caused pain, and made choices that hurt people who didn't deserve it. That made me culpable.

But forgiving myself? That was the real fight.

It wasn't about pretending I didn't do wrong. It was about creating boundaries and finally understanding how trauma and years of chaos had shaped me into the man I was becoming. I had to face the truth that I was deeply self-destructive. It wasn't just circumstance—it was something wired into my DNA. Somewhere in my foundation, I had been programmed to believe I wasn't good enough. That belief became the script that played over every decision, every relationship, every fall.

People love to say, "Love yourself." But that's not how it works. You can't jump straight to love without first accepting yourself. Before you can love who you are, you have to sit with the parts that make you uncomfortable—the shame, the scars, the failures—and stop running from them. You have to understand your patterns, your triggers, your demons. Then, you have to respect yourself enough not to feed them anymore.

There were periods of my life when I didn't just dislike myself—I hated myself. In college, I hit one of those dark stretches where I felt like there was no way out. I held a gun to my head once. Another time, I took a bottle of pills, ready to check out completely. Something about lying on that hospital bed, stomach pumped, organs failing, and the look on the nurse's face—somewhere between disgust and mercy—made me rethink that decision later.

I realized then that my issues ran deeper than I'd ever imagined. The abuse, the anger, the loss—they had all carved grooves into my brain that replayed the same old story: You're not enough. But I started to see that the only way out was through. I had to take control, not of the world around me, but of the world inside me. And that first step was understanding my path—why I became who I was, and what I had to do to stop being a prisoner of it.

In college, I took psychology courses that, at the time, I thought were just electives. Funny how life brings lessons back around when you need them. One theory that stuck with me was that forgiveness isn't an emotion—it's a cognitive decision. It's not about forgetting or condoning; it's about releasing yourself from the mental prison of resentment. Psychologists say holding onto guilt or anger keeps the brain in a constant state of stress. The amygdala—the part that triggers fight or flight—never turns off. You live in survival mode, unable to heal.

I learned that forgiveness actually reprograms the brain. It activates areas tied to empathy, compassion, and emotional regulation. Over time, that rewiring creates peace—not by erasing what happened, but by stripping it of its power over you.

So, I started forgiving—not to let people off the hook, but to let myself off the leash. I stopped waiting for apologies that were never coming and stopped punishing myself for who I used to be.

Forgiveness wasn't about becoming perfect. It was about becoming free.

A Psychologist's Perspective on Redemption

From a psychologist's standpoint, redemption isn't just a moral or emotional journey—it's a neurological one. The process of rebuilding yourself after years of trauma, addiction, or destructive behavior is quite literally a rewiring of the brain.

When a person experiences prolonged chaos—abuse, substance use, rage, or self-sabotage—the brain adapts to survive in that environment. It builds pathways that reinforce danger, pleasure, and impulsive decisions. Over time, those pathways become your default wiring. You don't even realize it's happening because the mind is trying to protect itself from pain, even when that protection becomes the problem.

According to trauma psychologists, recovery is not about "forgetting" the past but integrating it. The goal isn't to erase what happened—it's to teach your nervous system that the danger is over. Every moment of discipline, every refusal to relapse, every time you confront a trigger without reacting, you're teaching your brain a new pattern of safety.

Forgiveness, self-awareness, and healthy boundaries are more than spiritual ideas; they're neurological training. By consciously choosing empathy, gratitude, and accountability, you stimulate the prefrontal cortex—the part of the brain responsible for decision-making, regulation, and long-term planning. Over time, those new habits can actually shrink the influence of the amygdala, which controls fear and emotional reactivity.

In short, redemption is both psychological and physiological. Healing isn't just about changing your behavior; it's about changing your biology. And the beauty is—science proves it's possible. Neuroplasticity shows that the brain can rewire itself at any age. That means no matter how deep the pit, there's always a way out if you keep climbing.

The Self-Help Section – Building Your Own Stairway

Redemption isn't magic. It's math. Steps, stacked daily. Here's the stairway I climbed—and you can too:

1. Acknowledge the Pit. Stop lying. If your life is a mess, admit it. The hardest step is saying, I am not okay.
2. Find the First Step. Don't think about the whole staircase. Just find one thing you can do today. Skip the drink. Block the number. Go to the gym.
3. Replace the Poison. If you don't replace the addiction with purpose, the addiction will come back. Fill the space with something that feeds you.
4. Reps Over Results. You won't feel better overnight. But every "no" to chaos is a rep toward strength.
5. Face the Ghosts. Temptation won't vanish. Learn to stare it down. Remind yourself of the pit, then keep climbing.
6. Forgive to Free Yourself. Resentment is a backpack full of bricks. Drop it if you want to make it up the stairs.
7. Build Daily Discipline. Redemption is boring. It's routine. It's doing the work even when nobody claps for you.

Closing Reflection

My staircase wasn't polished marble. It was jagged, broken, and covered in blood. But every scar was proof that I kept climbing.

And if you're reading this, I promise—your staircase is there too. You just have to take the first step.

Figure 1. 1973–1974 — My mom holding me upright, my brother by her side. Her eyes tell a story of strength, struggle, and unconditional love.

Figure 2. 1973–1974 My mom, dad, brother and my angel and grandmother, Agnes. How fitting her name also, the name of a historical saint!

Figure 3. The irony of the tear above me says it all — my brother was forced by Sears to stand close. Two boys, one camera, and a moment that told a much bigger story.

Figure 4. I got good at hiding the pain—until the day I couldn't anymore. That's when everything changed.

Figure 5. I wore strength like armor and silence like a shield. But when the worst happened, both shattered.

Figure 6. For years, I was good at covering the pain, smiling through the ache like it was second nature. But then the worst happened—and there was no more hiding. That moment didn't just break me; it began to rebuild me.

Figure 7. For years, I built walls around the pain. But when the storm came, even the strongest walls gave way.

Figure 8. Christmas Day, captured in stillness. We played the part of a happy family, pretending everything was fine. When I rediscovered this photo, I showed it to my wife, Trisha, and said, "This is it—this is when my eyes said what my voice never could."

Figure 9. My mother at 20 years old — damaged and scared, but still standing. The kind of strength no one should have to learn that young.

Figure 10. Grandpa Ray in California — standing in a moment that feels like yesterday. There was something steady about him, a kind of peace that made the world slow down. He didn't say much, but when he did, you listened.

Figure 11. Grandpa Ray — California days, endless stories, and a lifetime of lessons in his smile.

Figure 12. Grandpa Ray and Grandma Margaret with my dad and his sister — the generations that built the world I was born into. You can see both love and survival in their faces. What they carried, they passed down. And what I carry now, I'm determined to heal.

Figure 13. This was the last picture taken of Grandpa Ray before he took his own life. Looking back, I can see it now — how death wears a calm disguise. His eyes weren't empty; they were full of everything he could no longer carry. I didn't understand it then, but now I know — the soul often says goodbye long before the body does.

Figure 14. My father and me at my first wedding, 2000. On the surface, everything looked in place. But behind the smile, I was fighting chaos no one could see.

Figure 15. My dad and his girlfriend Toni at my wedding. Everyone looked happy that day, but even then, there were unspoken stories behind every smile.

Figure 16. My brother and my first dog — the one constant of my childhood. That dog wasn't just loyal; he was a lifeline. When the world felt unsafe, he stood between me and the storm, protecting me not just physically, but emotionally, in ways I didn't recognize

Figure 17. My mom and dad with their closest friends, Ron and Glenda — their go-to couple for every party and every pour. Back then, it looked like friendship and fun. Now I realize it was more about drowning pain than celebrating life. Still, for a while, laughter echoed louder than the hurt.

Figure 18. Running the ball — needed 4, got 14. That's how I played the game and lived life: push through, keep your balance, and don't stop till you've earned extra yards. Back when cable was really cable... and somehow, life felt clearer on that field.

Figure 19. Brunswick Blue Devils — Pioneer Conference Champions, 1992. My final year. All-State, All-Conference, All-Star. The kind of season you never forget — when every hit, every yard, and every ounce of work finally meant something.

Figure 20. 1991, my junior year. Steroids ruled my world. I told myself it was about performance, about being unstoppable. But deep down, it was about control — over a life that felt anything but. I built armor to hide the damage, never realizing that every shot, every pill, was just another layer of pain I'd have to peel back years later.

Figure 21. Sam and Val — two souls who showed up when I needed quiet love the most. They remind me every day that healing often comes with four paws and a wagging tail.

Figure 22. December 13, 2015 — our wedding day on the coast of Florida. I remember the salt in the air, the way the waves crashed behind us, and how she looked at me like she already knew every part I tried to hide. I was still running from myself, still wearing my masks. But Trisha saw the man I could become, not just the one I was. Ten years later, in 2025, she's still here — loving me through the wreckage, believing in the redemption I once doubted was possible.

Figure 23. Washington D.C. — the night I stood on stage accepting Entrepreneur of the Year and Wall Street Businessman of the Year. I shook hands, posed for photos, smiled like I had it all figured out. But inside, I was falling apart. It's strange how the higher you climb, the better you get at hiding the fall.

Figure 24. This was the moment everything should've ended — the truck rolled, the chaos caught up, and I should've been gone and risked my wife's life. But somehow, we walked away. I don't call that luck. I call it mercy. God wasn't done with us yet.

Figure 25. It was 2025, after a business meeting in Manhattan. My wife and I sat back, a cigar burning slow between thoughts and laughter. For the first time in decades, peace didn't feel like something I had to chase. I was 80% done with the book then — and I realized I wasn't just writing about redemption. I was living it.

Chapter 10:
The Power of Entrepreneurship

"Building a business saved my life—because it gave my pain a purpose."

Some kids build sandcastles. I built escape routes.

While most twelve-year-olds were worried about video games and cartoons, I was writing contracts and raking leaves. Every snow day wasn't a break—it was a business opportunity. I'd lace up my boots, grab my shovel, and hit the icy driveways of Cleveland Heights. At that age, I was already cashing $500 checks and racking up nearly $7,000 in seasonal work—and not because I liked the cold. It was survival. Every dollar I made gave me one more reason to stay away from the hell I called home.

My first real taste of entrepreneurship wasn't in a boardroom. It was in the magic section of Starship Earth, a wild little shop in the late '80s where I sold fake college IDs, magic tricks, knives, and whatever bizarre product Steve—the eccentric owner—cooked up that week. It was part horror movie, part hustle, and all adrenaline. I studied Houdini and horror films not for entertainment, but for escape. Magic was survival. Illusions were therapy. And every prank or sale I made felt like I was controlling something in a life where I had controlled nothing.

Broke, but Never Broken

By college, I was broke like every other student—but I had already tasted financial independence, and I couldn't un-taste it. I took a bus across town with nothing but cologne on and a lie in my mouth. I told Ganley I was a seasoned salesman. Truth was, I was just a hungry kid who had been hustling since I could hold a rake. They hired me, gave me a car, and I never looked back.

Then came my biggest bluff: the day I shook hands with Lee Siedman—billionaire owner of Motorcars Group—at the IX Center. I lied through my teeth, told him I was a finance manager. I wasn't. But I became one overnight. My first day I showed up before sunrise, clueless, scared out of my mind. I didn't even know how to print the damn forms. But I figured it out. I created my own process folders, mapped out the print menus, learned what each bank preferred, and made it my mission to be the cleanest, most efficient closer on the floor. I arrived on a lie—but I stayed on grit.

When you've been numb for most of your childhood, fear becomes fuel. My back was always against the wall, but I'd been living in corners my whole life. The stakes of failure didn't scare me—because I had already survived worse.

Scaling Pain into Purpose

That mindset propelled me into building a multimillion-dollar empire. I started an extended service contract company out of Kinkos. No investors. No tech team. Just me, my grit, and a pile of printed contracts. I hit the phones, hit the streets, worked deals, ran promos, and built relationships. I sent finance managers on cruises as incentives. I became a vendor-of-choice. And when I tapped into my inner nerd and filed patents for a paperless service platform, I landed banks and manufacturers on contracts that changed the game.

By 24, I was earning more than most grown men. I had luxury cars, custom suits, jewelry—and a mountain of unresolved trauma hiding behind it all. I thought I had made it. But here's what nobody tells you: money amplifies who you already are. Power doesn't heal pain—

it magnifies it. And beneath my success, the emotional cracks were starting to widen.

Entrepreneurship gave me purpose. It gave my pain a home. But it also revealed the work I hadn't done on myself. I was a keynote speaker, a dealmaker in D.C., an industry innovator—but inside, I was still that kid dodging fists and searching for something to believe in.

Business Is a Team Sport (What Football and the Military Teach You)

Entrepreneurship aligns with sports—and even the military—more than most people realize. The lessons are the same: unity, clear roles, ruthless prep, and watching each other's six. Football taught me that brotherhood isn't a slogan; it's a standard. You lift the man next to you. You communicate. You hold the line when it's fourth and inches. Business is no different.

Some of my closest friendships weren't forged in locker rooms—they were forged in boardrooms and showrooms. The pressure, the pace, the need to execute under heat—it builds a bond the same way two-a-days do. You learn who folds and who finishes. You learn who plays for stats and who plays for the team.

Wichita: Culture, Turnaround, and a Lifelong Teammate

One of those friendships is with **Dr. Cassell**—the same man who penned this book's foreword. He was the finance manager at a Subaru store where I was hired as general manager to fix a mess. That job moved me from Cleveland to **Wichita, Kansas**, and the place had a familiar feel—**Brunstucky** energy: a good-old-boy network running the show, and only two Black staff members in the entire dealership. You could smell the culture problem as soon as you walked the floor.

I don't care in business what color you are or who you love. I care if you can perform and if you live the standard. I found the cancers quick—dead weight, protected by proximity to the owner, people who confused tenure with value. I gutted the place and led from the front. I fired the owner's close friend and a family member, because the job demands courage, not courtesy. You don't fix a culture by taping it together. You cut out the rot and you build new muscle.

Dr. Cassell was bright—surgical in his thinking—and I picked up on it immediately. He became a crucial prong in the turnaround. We meshed. We could see the play before it unfolded, finish each other's next moves in F&I and on the desk. We rebuilt process, pricing discipline, and trust. I was proud of the work and proud of the team we built.

To this day, I'm on him to open a new-car store with me in Florida. I'll get him there—I'm relentless—and we both know we'd win.

The moral: put aside the noise—politics, race, identity—and evaluate people by performance, character, and growth. Invest in the ones who invest in the mission. I've always taken stock of people because I'm built from pain—and I'm standing here because others invested in me. Their belief was louder than my abusers. That's why my inner circle, including Dr. Cassell, tells me what I **need** to hear, not what I **want** to hear. Real teammates do that.

Rebuilding From Rock Bottom

After serving 13 months of my 16-month sentence, I was released early with good time and credits earned from tutoring 35 inmates to earn their GEDs. That was a real milestone I remain proud of. I didn't sit there and cry, "poor me." I was responsible for my actions, justified or not.

The day I walked out, my wife picked me up with my dog, who missed me dearly. I broke down crying, not because I was free—but because I had to face her, and face it all. I had only $140 to my name. That was my restart.

I called Chris, borrowed $500, fixed my car, and sold it. That cash became the seed money to start what is now my dealership and auto repair shop—right in the middle of COVID-19. Not exactly a prime time to launch a business, but I had one thing on my side: rest. I had been still for over a year. My mind was sharp. My drive was relentless.

I didn't let shame kill me. I let purpose wake me back up.

A Psychologist's Perspective: The Healing Power of Enterprise

From a clinical psychology standpoint, entrepreneurship—especially for trauma survivors—can function as a vital therapeutic outlet. For individuals like me, who endured childhood abuse, control was stolen at a young age. Rebuilding control through business creation allows the brain to experience empowerment, purpose, and identity reconstruction.

Studies have shown that survivors of trauma often develop a heightened sensitivity to risk and detail. These traits, when channeled appropriately, can become entrepreneurial superpowers. Business becomes not just an income source, but a vehicle for mastery, emotional regulation, and self-worth.

In college, I unknowingly reinforced this therapeutic model. My grind wasn't just for grades—it was for survival, dignity, and internal recalibration. While I didn't sit in a therapy circle, I processed my pain through the structure of school, the discipline of sports, and the hustle of business. I learned that a GPA couldn't heal wounds, but achievement could build scaffolding around the damage.

When I studied behavioral psychology, it made sense in reverse: my hyper-awareness, distrust, perfectionism—all textbook traits of trauma survivors. But I also discovered that with guidance, these traits could be flipped into empathy, leadership, and clarity under pressure. College taught me more than business. It taught me how to study myself, question my defaults, and start rewriting my internal operating system.

"From survival hustles to building businesses- earning money doesn't heal pain."

The First Hustle

My first taste of entrepreneurship didn't come with a business license, a ribbon cutting, or applause. It came from survival.

When you grow up in chaos, money isn't luxury—it's control. It's the one thing that lets you breathe in a world that keeps trying to choke you.

I sold candy at school. Cut lawns. Flipped sneakers before it was a thing. Every dollar I made meant freedom. Every sale was a small rebellion against the chaos I was born into.

This will most likely be the longest chapter—business is something I adore as much as football. It's competitive. Tell me I can't do it? Fuck you—watch me. That mindset has been my fuel since day one.

But survival hustles don't teach you stability. They teach you speed. They teach you how to react, not how to build. And that wiring—fast, restless, hungry—would later become both my gift and my curse.

From Hustles to Empires

As I got older, the hustles turned into businesses. I wasn't just chasing money anymore—I was chasing identity.

Auto shops. Car dealerships. Warranty companies. Sports management. Consulting and marketing firms. Real estate. I had a knack for taking something small and making it big, and I understood the operational side of sustainability. To this day, I don't know how that manifested, but I cherish it daily.

I was a deal-making machine, and on the outside, it looked like I'd won.

But the truth was, I'd only built a bigger cage—with better furniture.

Every success was a distraction from the truth I didn't want to face. I wasn't building for love or legacy—I was building to prove I was enough.

Anger as My CEO

Business was my therapy, but I didn't realize I was feeding my illness instead of curing it.

I made deals to prove people wrong. I signed contracts out of spite. I spent money to flex, not to build. If someone doubted me, I made sure they'd never do it again.

But anger doesn't manage employees. Ego doesn't balance the books. Rage doesn't read contracts.

And slowly, my companies became battlefields. Employees didn't know if they'd meet the businessman or the brawler. People couldn't trust me because I couldn't trust myself.

From a psychologist's point of view, anger became my engine because it was familiar. It was the emotion I had access to—the one that made me feel powerful instead of powerless. When you grow up in survival mode, anger becomes a shield. It creates the illusion of control and confidence, even when you're bleeding inside. The brain learns to associate anger with action, progress, and safety. The problem is, when anger drives the car, it eventually crashes. And in my case, anger wasn't just the fuel—it was still the boss.

That's the thing about entrepreneurship—your demons don't stay home. They clock in with you every day wearing your company logo.

Addiction in a Suit and Tie

People think addiction looks like a needle or a bottle. But addiction wears suits too.

Mine wore $3,000 custom Italian suits, paired with hand-stitched ties and crisp shirts adorned with mother-of-pearl buttons. I looked like the definition of success, but every stitch was holding together denial.

My therapist once told me, "You've mastered control in business because it's the only part of your life you can dominate. Your personal life—you avoid. You let it fall apart because you can't control people like you can control a business."

She was 100% right.

I had switched addictions—from chaos to control, from drugs to deals, from pain to profit. Building businesses became my drug. Each new venture was another hit of dopamine, another distraction from emptiness.

Therapists believe the visual image becomes crucial for someone who's dying inside because it's the last thing they can control. When the internal world is collapsing, the external one becomes armor. The appearance of perfection is a performance meant to distract from pain. It's a survival instinct—if you look successful, maybe you can convince yourself you're okay. It's the illusion of stability in the middle of emotional free fall.

And like any addiction, it escalated. The more money I made, the higher-end my sex partners became. When I was broke, I drove through dark streets looking for release—sometimes for $20, sometimes for the illusion of connection.

It wasn't about lust; it was about escape. It was about running from abuse, guilt, and reflection.

No woman, no deal, no dollar could fill the void. I was winning on paper and dying inside.

9/11 & My Collapse

"When the towers fell, so did I."

I thought it would never end. The McMansion in Brecksville. Four exotic cars in the driveway. Custom $3,000 suits. A Rolex on my wrist every morning, feeding the lie: *I am the man.*

Through all the hell I'd lived, I convinced myself I'd conquered it. I was young, sharp, unstoppable.

Then 9/11 hit.
And it hit hard.

Everything changed overnight. Business froze. Deals disappeared. People were scared to shake hands. The world had stopped turning the way it used to.

Back then, you didn't close deals over email or Zoom. You looked people in the eye, shook their hand, broke bread. After 9/11, that vanished. Fear replaced opportunity.

And when the economy shook, the media came hunting.

I became their story.

Political pushback. Tabloid headlines. Reporters camped outside. Federal investigators sniffing around. All of it started with a bottom-feeder rag built on escort ads and filth.

My face—smoking a cigar in my office—plastered across the front page. That photo came from an "Entrepreneur of the Year" interview I didn't even want to do. I told the photographer, "This feels cocky."

But my team convinced me. "It'll help your brand."

After a few drinks, I leaned back on the office couch, cigar in hand, looking like every arrogant businessman stereotype they could sell. I didn't know that photo would become my noose.

Ultimately, after deep investigation, I proved my case in court and no charges were filed against me. I fought the system—I called out their lies and exposed the crooks behind the scenes: judges, attorneys for the state, all looking for billable hours and empty memos. They weren't in the business of making the consumer whole; they were in the business of padding records.

They even tried to get a court order to remove me, but the judge found I was competent and doing a tremendous job restructuring the company. Still, they kept chasing me around town. Then one morning a 6 a.m. segment aired saying I was a Republican hobnobbing with President Bush and that Governor Jim Petro had no intention of doing anything about it, I knew I was fighting more than I could handle.

An ex-wife fueled by greed, sexual addiction spiraling out of control, and rage stacking its bricks—everything piled up. I even chased down the snowflake who wrote the article, driving at high speed, terrified and furious. I told him to keep fucking with me. He was scared— good. I wanted him to know what it felt like to be hunted.

My COO was diagnosed with cancer. He had a wife and kids. I cut him an exit check and terminated his employment. He told me I couldn't fight this alone. I told him I was done fighting. That was my choice—stop the chaos, nobody else.

In court, I snatched cameras, and in a moment of pure rage, I told the prosecutor I was coming over to fuck his wife. I was out of control; I caused the circus with my aggression. You do attract more bees with honey, and I was pissing on a hive of hornets daily. I was crazy—"crazy white boy" was a nickname I'd earned in the hood, and it even trickled into federal court.

The Whore Plug & The Sting

Even in the chaos of that collapse, I never let my addictions touch my work. My businesses stayed sharp. But my personal life? That was a slow-motion car crash.

I had a "plug"—a guy who ran a site touring women through town, dating men with demons like mine. He'd call me when someone new hit the circuit. "Got a stunner for you," he'd say.

One day he called, and I said I'd meet her at the hotel around noon—on my lunch break.

I walked into the room. As the door closed, I heard her whisper, "He's here."

My gut screamed, *turn around, get out.*

I said, "Sorry, wrong room," and turned to leave.

But before I could take another step, about seven undercover cops flooded the hallway—badges flashing, guns low, voices barking, "Get on the ground!"

I pleaded, "What's going on?" playing dumb.

They cuffed me and dragged me into an unmarked car just as news vans pulled up. "What's happening?" I kept asking.

One detective hit play on a recorder. There it was—my voice, talking to my connect about the girl.

I dropped my head. "I've got a wife and a little kid," I said. "Spare me. Our relationship is over. That's why I do this."

Which was true. At home, intimacy was dead. I was just a paycheck.

But if I'm honest, even if she'd been the perfect wife, I would've still found a way to mess it up.

From a psychologist's point of view, sexual addiction works just like any other addiction—it hijacks the brain's reward system. The dopamine rush that comes from the chase, the fantasy, the act—it creates a temporary sense of relief from pain, shame, or loneliness. But over time, the brain adapts and demands more stimulation to feel alive. The addiction isn't about sex—it's about escape. It's about controlling the uncontrollable, finding a momentary cure for emptiness. The cycle becomes brutal: craving, indulgence, guilt, shame, and back again.

That day in the hotel wasn't just a sting operation. It was a neurological collision between trauma and temptation—a wake-up call that I was losing myself one decision at a time.

The Rebuild

The day I got caught in that sting, I stopped lying to myself. I had turned my trauma into trophies and called it success. I was chasing highs in boardrooms and bedrooms, always trying to outrun the echo of pain.

I learned that control is an illusion. You can have everything—money, power, respect—and still be completely powerless over yourself.

That day forced me to start over—not just in business, but in life.

I slowed down. I started building with purpose. I began leading with honesty instead of ego.

I of course, fell down the stairs several times…

Purpose Over Profit

When I stopped chasing wealth and started chasing meaning, everything changed. I built businesses that lifted others. I gave second chances to people who needed them because I knew what it felt like to fall.

I learned that legacy isn't built on what you buy—it's built on what you give.

Entrepreneurship became more than a hustle. It became healing.

Money is a metric. Purpose is a compass.

Money tells you if the engine is running. Purpose tells you where to drive.

When I aimed only at revenue, I kept asking, *"How do we squeeze more?"*

When I centered purpose, I started asking, *"How do we serve better?"* The first question shrank my world to monthly targets; the second widened it to the lives that those numbers touched.

The shift didn't make me less ambitious. It made me more precise. Profit became an outcome, not the point. And ironically, outcomes improved—customers stayed longer, partners leaned in, and my team brought energy I could never buy with bonuses alone.

Purpose changes the *feel* of the work

- **Energy:** Work fueled by purpose returns energy instead of draining it. You end hard days tired, not empty.

- **Resilience:** Setbacks stop being verdicts. They're feedback. When the "why" is bigger than the bad day, you return tomorrow.

- **Trust:** People can feel whether you're using them or building with them. Purpose compounds into reputation, and reputation compounds into opportunity.

- **Focus:** You stop chasing every shiny idea. Purpose becomes a filter that cuts distractions and clarifies the few moves that matter.

Giving second chances changed our culture

Early on, I made a simple promise: we would bet on people others overlooked—nonlinear résumés, career gaps, past mistakes. Not blindly, but boldly.
When you build a company that believes people can grow, the culture learns to coach instead of label. Performance improves because people feel seen. Accountability strengthens because it's anchored in dignity, not fear. The result is a team that works like owners, not renters.

Purpose didn't make our standards soft. It made them meaningful. We measured what mattered: effort, learning, improvement, and the value created for customers. That created a different kind of pride—the kind you carry home.

A simple model: The Purpose Flywheel

1. **Purpose clarifies who you serve and why.**

2. **Clarity shapes decisions.** You say "yes" faster and "no" more often.

3. **Better decisions build trust.** With customers, partners, and your team.

4. **Trust drives performance.** Referrals rise, churn falls, execution tightens.

5. **Performance funds the mission.** Profit becomes fuel, not a finish line.

6. **Fuel reinvested deepens purpose.** And the cycle accelerates.

Round by round, that flywheel spins faster than any growth hack.

The three-question decision filter

Before pursuing an opportunity, we started asking:

1. **Does this help the people we're here to serve?**

2. **Does this grow the kind of leader I want to become?**

3. **If it succeeds, will we be proud of how we got there?**

If we couldn't answer "yes" to all three, the opportunity was noise, not signal—even if it looked profitable.

Metrics that money can't measure (but you should)

- **Customer gratitude:** Not just NPS—collect real stories of solved problems.

- **Quality of hires:** Are the right people seeking *you* out?

- **Depth of partnerships:** Are partners voluntarily bringing you into bigger rooms?

- **Learning velocity:** How quickly do we discover, decide, and improve?

- **Reputation lag:** What positive thing do people say about you when you're not in the room?

Track these alongside revenue. Profit tells you *how loud* the business is. These tell you *what song* it's playing.

Purpose is not charity—it's strategy

Purpose doesn't excuse sloppy execution or unsustainable pricing. It sharpens both. You price fairly because you plan to be here for your customers in ten years. You design processes that respect people's time—clients and team alike. You protect margins because stability is a gift to everyone who depends on the business.

And when profit and purpose feel in tension, you get creative. You look for the third path—simplify the offer, narrow the niche, redesign the experience. Constraints force craft.

What purpose did for me

Purpose helped me rebuild after my own stumbles. It gave me permission to be honest about my limits and to ask for help. It turned "I have to" into "I get to." I stopped counting wins by what I could show off and started counting by who I could lift up. The work became quieter and richer. The scoreboard mattered, but the stories mattered more.

How to operationalize purpose (today)

- **Write it in a sentence:** *We exist to ____ for ____ so they can ____.* Keep revising until it fits on a sticky note.

- **Design one "signature" act of service:** Something small you do for every customer that proves what you believe.

- **Stand up a Second-Chance Pipeline:** Commit a slice of your hiring to overlooked talent. Pair it with coaching and clear standards.

- **Close the loop with stories:** Start meetings with a 60-second story of someone helped by your work. Stories keep the mission real.

- **Set a "no" quota:** Each quarter, track how many misaligned opportunities you turned down. Celebrate those decisions.

- **Reinvest intentionally:** Earmark a percentage of profit to deepen your mission—training, community partnerships, or customer experience.

Legacy is built in the ordinary

Most legacy isn't a grand gesture. It's the daily decision to do right by people: returning a call, paying on time, owning a mistake, giving credit, telling the truth. Purpose lives in those moments. Over time they stack into something heavy enough to hand to the next person.

The quiet payoff

Money can solve a lot of problems, but it can't answer the questions that wake you at 2 a.m. Purpose can. It tells you why you're carrying the weight and who benefits when you don't quit. It makes the long road worth walking and the short wins worth less.

When I stopped chasing wealth and started chasing meaning, I didn't abandon profit. I put it in its proper place. Money became a great servant. Purpose stayed the master.

Entrepreneurship became more than a hustle. It became healing—and that pays in ways a bank account never will.

A Psychologist's Perspective on This Chapter

From a clinical standpoint, this chapter is a study in conversion—how trauma transforms into drive, and how pain disguises itself as productivity.

Psychologists often see men who use work, wealth, or sex as coping mechanisms rather than goals. These external pursuits give structure and control in a world that once felt unsafe and chaotic.

For trauma survivors, success becomes a substitute for safety—and ambition becomes armor.

Entrepreneurship, in that sense, can be both medicine and poison. The same neural circuits that drive innovation also feed addiction. Dopamine—the brain's reward chemical—doesn't care if it's triggered by closing a business deal or chasing a destructive thrill. To the mind in survival mode, both feel like victory.

Anger becomes the engine. Achievement becomes anesthesia. And control becomes the illusion that keeps the system alive.

True healing begins when a person learns that peace and power aren't the same thing. The real breakthrough isn't another business or another win—it's the ability to sit in stillness without collapsing.

Self-Help Lessons – What Entrepreneurship Really Teaches

1. **Money won't heal wounds.** It buys comfort, not peace.

2. **Control is an illusion.** The tighter you grip it, the faster it slips.

3. **Your business mirrors your mind.** Heal the operator, and the operation follows.

4. **Don't let anger lead.** Rage might build fast, but it burns faster.

5. **Addiction hides behind ambition.** Success can be a drug that kills slower.

6. **Failure isn't fatal—it's feedback.** Every collapse teaches something.

7. **Purpose outlasts profit.** Ego fades. Impact endures.

8. **Protect your circle.** The wrong people bankrupt your peace before your wallet.

9. **Legacy over lifestyle.** What you build for others lasts longer than what you buy for yourself.

10. **Redemption takes work.** Rebuilding your business is easy—rebuilding yourself is where the real fight begins.

Reflection – The Real Power

Entrepreneurship gave me everything—and took everything to test me.

It exposed my demons, magnified my flaws, and forced me to rebuild from the inside out. But it also gave me something priceless: the realization that I could rise again.

When I lost everything, I found the one thing that couldn't be taken from me—the will to rebuild.

That's the real power of entrepreneurship.

It's not about owning companies. It's about owning your story.

Anthony James Hodel

Chapter 11:
Fathers & Final Goodbyes

"Watching my father fade was like watching time itself run out—slow, unstoppable, and cruel."

My grandmother was so dear to me. I was out of state at college football camp when she passed and couldn't make it back. I never got to say goodbye. Over the years, I've visited her grave countless times—just sitting there, talking to her, like she could still hear me. Maybe she does. I see her in my dreams sometimes, the same warm smile, the same calm in her eyes. I like to think she still watches over me, making sure that even now, I'm trying to secure peace in my life.

She taught me what real love looked like—steady, patient, forgiving. The kind of love that didn't keep score. And I tested that love in one of the worst ways: in college, I took one of her checks, made it out to cash for $600, and used it to buy steroids. Addiction will, in fact, make you do anything for a "high." I've begged her forgiveness more times than I can count. If she were here, I think she would have told me what she always did—not that it was okay, but that I was still loved and capable of better. So, I keep trying to be better, to make amends where I can, to live in a way that would make her proud.

She gave me the same feeling my dogs do: pure, unconditional love without judgment. Losing her was my first lesson in absence—the ache of wanting one more conversation, one more hug. When I sit by her headstone now, I promise her that I'm still learning, still choosing honesty and peace, still carrying her love forward.

Steel, Summers & Scars

I only saw my grandfather in the summers until my early teens, but he treated me like a grown man long before I was one. He pushed me—hard—and he's the one who introduced me to the weight room. That mattered. In a world I couldn't control, he handed me iron and said, *Lift*.

In high school, I called him often. He came to Ohio for a few of my games, proud and loud in the stands. Then, in college, something shifted. His mental health started to fray. I'll never forget our last call—he didn't know who I was or why I was calling. The line went quiet in a way I can still hear.

He moved to New Mexico—the irony wasn't lost on me, given the way *Mexico* echoed through other chapters of my life. Then one day the phone rang, and the news took the air out of me: he had died by suicide. He'd prepared his shed, left a note, and used a gun.

Mental health has run rampant through my life. I saw his anger and his abuse as a kid; I also saw the pain behind it. I thank God that while I have my own trauma and issues to work through, I've turned the ship to a better course—and this book is part of that navigation. Get help if you need it. If you know someone who's suffering, they aren't weak. The mind is a powerful computer, and sometimes the wiring is off. Take a cry for help seriously.

My Mother's Death

My mother's death was different. I was prepared. I saw it coming. I even called it. Christmas of 2004, I visited her with my fiancée and saw her for about fifteen minutes—that was the way it had been for years. Her mental health had deteriorated so badly that it was hard to reach her.

I remember the last time we sat together for lunch and actually had a meaningful conversation. The woman who once carried over three hundred pounds was now a frail shadow, barely one hundred and twenty. She looked exhausted—tired of fighting. What I didn't know at the time was that she was living in an abusive relationship with a controlling man. I would later find out she had secretly married him. That fact stayed hidden until her death revealed it.

At that lunch, I told her, "Mom, move out. I'll pay for a car and an apartment. You don't have to live like this." She smiled weakly and said, "I'm okay."

That Christmas, I made it a point to tell her I appreciated her efforts—that I saw her, that I understood she had done her best to raise me right. I didn't tell her about the abuse my brother inflicted on me, or how it shaped my anger. I only apologized for putting her through hell. I told her, "You raised a good man." She brought up my long, drawn-out divorce, which ultimately dragged on for seven grueling years—like a bankruptcy case that wouldn't end.

When I left her house that day, I got into my car and was hit by a wave of dread so strong it almost felt audible. A voice inside me said, *Go back in. Talk to her again. You won't see her again.* I brushed it off, convincing myself I was just being emotional. A few weeks later, in January of 2005, she took her own life with a gun.

What came after still feels like a bad dream. My brother and I hadn't spoken in years, and I found out through others that I was banned from the funeral. They said I caused her death. I remember saying, "Are you fucking kidding me?" She had told people that I harassed her, that I called daily to hang up, that I was tormenting her because I had "picked my dad's side."

That couldn't have been further from the truth. I didn't pick sides. I just tried to hold relationships with both parents. I couldn't pick new ones, and despite everything, I still loved them both. I took the good from each and tried to understand the rest. My college psychology courses gave me a map to start healing—to understand trauma instead of drowning in it.

When I called the funeral home, they confirmed it was a private service arranged by her husband—and yes, I was on the "do not admit" list. That hit harder than any punch I'd ever taken.

I called an old friend, Patrick Byer, who was then the police chief of Brunswick and the father of one of my high school teammates. I asked, "Can they legally keep me from my own mother's funeral?" He sighed and said, "Yes, they can. But if you show up, we'll take our time responding when they call." The station was only two minutes away. "Just promise me," he said, "when it happens—leave in peace."

I promised I would. I just wanted to say goodbye.

I even called the funeral director and asked, "Can I at least see her before the service, while you're preparing her?" He told me gently, "She's in no condition for you to view. You don't want that to be your last memory of her."

That night, I left a voicemail for my brother—furious, shaking, raw. "Motherfucker, what you've put me through, and now this? You better call me or I'm coming out with the truth." He called back. I recorded the call while my fiancée sat next to me in the car, listening to every word. I told him, "Either I'm there, or everyone finds out what's really been going on." He begged me not to. "I'll lose my family," he said. I didn't care.

In the end, I was there. I stood as a pallbearer for my mother—something that should have never required a fight. That should've been a given.

After the burial, we stood at her gravesite and talked for the first time in years. We pieced together the painful truth: our mother had pitted us against each other, spinning lies and drama to create a wedge between her sons. I thought maybe that day could be a new beginning for us. We made peace on the surface, but the scars he left on me—those never healed.

That loss, that chaos, that betrayal—it reshaped how I viewed death. It wasn't just the end of life; it was the unraveling of family secrets, of unspoken pain, of everything we never had the courage to say out loud.

So when I say watching my father fade was like watching time itself run out—slow, unstoppable, and cruel—it carried the weight of **three losses**. One I saw coming. One I didn't. And one that arrived like a storm that had been building for years.

It doesn't hit you all at once. At first, it's small things—forgetfulness, fatigue, a man who once carried weight like a warrior suddenly struggling with steps. I wanted to believe it was temporary. That he'd bounce back. But denial is the first lie we tell ourselves when we're staring at mortality.

I still remember the first time I had to help my father out of a chair. It shook me. The man who once towered over me with a belt now leaned on me for balance. The roles had flipped, and in that moment I realized the power dynamic of my entire life had shifted.

Here's the truth: for most of my life, the bottle was more important to my father than I was. From birth until I was well into my thirties, he was absent. He never held my hand. Never tucked me in. Never told me I was enough. And I carried that anger—deep, hot, and heavy. I wondered why I didn't get the father who showed up at games, who taught his son to fish, who said, "I love you." Instead, I got distance. I got silence. I got a man lost in the bottom of a bottle.

But what I know today is this: he never had it done for him either. He didn't have a blueprint for love or fatherhood. He did the best he could with what he had. That doesn't excuse it, but it explains it. And in those final days, I started to let go of the blame.

Illness is a thief that doesn't kick in the door—it sneaks in, bit by bit. One day he could walk to the kitchen; the next, it was a battle just to get to the bathroom. The hardest part wasn't watching his body fail—it was watching his spirit dim. My father was proud, strong, and stubborn. To see him surrender to weakness felt like watching a giant crumble.

I kept pushing him to fight, to walk, to eat, to keep going. But deep down, I knew I wasn't just fighting for him—I was fighting my own fear of losing him.

When the end drew near, something happened that I never thought I'd get. I held his hand. And this time—he held mine back. In that moment, decades of anger started to loosen. It was like the bad days died with him. I realized I had been waiting for that single gesture my whole life: proof that he saw me, proof that I mattered. And though it came at the very end, it was enough to start healing the boy inside me who always wondered why he wasn't enough.

As he slipped away, I prayed over him with the chaplain. I didn't know what my father's faith truly was—if he ever believed, if he ever prayed himself. But in that room, something shifted. The chaplain spent another forty minutes with me afterward. He told me, "You stayed. You gave him what he wanted—to die at home, not in a home. That matters."

Then he said something that cut straight through me: "You forgave him. Imagine what God will do."

In that moment, the child in me—the one who carried all that hurt and rage—finally pushed the damaged tears out. And when I let them fall, I felt the weight lift. The pain that had been welded to me for decades began to loosen, and what replaced it was quiet, heavy peace.

But not every moment was peaceful. In those last years, my father could be… a handful. He'd call me for every little thing. The battery in his remote. The TV not turning on. Ordering food from his favorite takeout spot. I used to answer those calls half-frustrated, half-joking—"Man, you sure need me for everything!" I'd laugh but underneath it, I was worn thin.

At times I'd think, *How did this man who once ignored me now need me for every breath?* But life has a twisted sense of irony. The same father who once felt unreachable now reached out daily—and I didn't always appreciate it the way I should have.

His longtime girlfriend, Toni, was an angel. She waited on him for over thirty years, hand and foot. She spoiled him, really. And he got used to that level of attention. So when she wasn't around, I was the next one on deck. He'd call me as if I were his personal assistant, not his son. And sometimes, I'd lose patience.

Today, months after his death, I'd give anything for one more of those calls. I'd give anything to hear his voice asking me to order him his favorite pepper steak or to help him figure out which button changed the TV input. Back then, I saw those moments as interruptions. Now, I see them for what they were—time. Time I can't get back.

Funny how what once felt like inconvenience turns into the very thing you ache to experience again. I'd give anything to order him that meal one more time, just to talk a little longer, to laugh about something meaningless.

Grief does that—it flips the lens. The things that once frustrated you become the things you'd do anything to have again.

The final days were the hardest. Sitting in that room, listening to the machines, feeling the air so heavy you could cut it. When the end came, it wasn't loud. It was quiet. A slow exhale, and then nothing. The silence that followed was the loudest sound I've ever heard.

My goodbye wasn't polished or pretty. It was raw: "I love you. Thank you. I forgive you." And for the first time, I meant it.

Losing my father forced me to confront my own life. You spend your youth thinking time is unlimited. You hustle, grind, chase money, chase women, chase validation. Then you watch someone you love take their last breath, and it changes everything. I realized that money can't buy more time. Power can't stop the clock. Anger, addiction, ego—they all look meaningless when you're holding a hand that's turning cold.

Mortality is the great equalizer. It humbles kings and criminals alike.

Lessons I Learned the Hard Way

- **Time is the real currency.** You can make money back. You can't make time back. Spend it wisely.

- **Presence over performance.** Sometimes your loved ones don't need you to fix things—they just need you to be there.

- **Say the words now.** Don't wait for the funeral to say "I love you," "I forgive you," or "I'm sorry." Dead ears can't hear apologies.

- **Forgiveness is freedom.** Carrying hate doesn't punish them—it poisons you. Let it go before it's too late.

- **Live with intention.** Watching death up close should be a reminder to live. Not just exist. Not just grind. Actually live.

- **Take cries for help seriously.** Struggle isn't weakness. It's a signal. Answer it with compassion and action.

Psychologist's Perspective: The Healing Power of Closure and Forgiveness

From a clinical standpoint, the experiences described in this chapter reflect what psychologists call **ambiguous grief**—a form of mourning tied to relationships marked by both love and pain. When a parent (or grandparent) is emotionally unavailable or abusive, the grieving process becomes layered. You aren't just mourning the person who died; you're mourning the caregiver you never had.

Forgiveness, in this sense, isn't about excusing harm. It's about reclaiming emotional agency. Research in trauma psychology shows that forgiveness—when it grows from self-awareness, not denial—can lower stress hormones, ease depression, and restore emotional regulation.

Watching a parent decline can also reopen childhood wounds. The adult caregiver is suddenly faced with the powerless child inside them. But when that adult chooses compassion instead of resentment, the brain literally rewires. Neural imaging studies reveal that empathy and forgiveness activate the same centers that process safety and connection. In other words, compassion heals what anger corrodes.

In this chapter, my journey illustrates **earned secure attachment**: the ability to create emotional safety internally, even if it was never modeled externally. Holding my father's hand became both a literal and psychological act of integration—where grief, love, and understanding finally met.

Self-Help Section:
Dealing with the Loss of a Family Member

Grief isn't linear. It's not a process you complete—it's a language you learn to live with. Losing a parent, grandparent, sibling, or loved one can create waves of guilt, anger, and confusion that come and go without warning. Here's what helped me—and might help you too:

1. **Allow Yourself to Feel Everything.** Don't rush the pain. Don't bottle it. You can't heal what you refuse to feel.

2. **Find Your Ritual.** Whether it's visiting a grave, lighting a candle, or writing them a letter—ritual gives your grief structure.

3. **Don't Judge Your Timeline.** People will tell you to "move on." Don't. Move forward. Healing doesn't erase—it transforms.

4. **Speak to Them.** Say what you never said. In your car, in your dreams, at their resting place. Connection doesn't end with death—it changes form.

5. **Channel the Pain into Purpose.** Honor them through action—volunteer, create, forgive, or simply live better. Let your pain fuel growth.

6. **Seek Support When Needed.** There's no shame in therapy, grief counseling, or leaning on friends. Isolation builds walls; connection builds bridges.

7. **If someone may be at risk, act.** Ask directly, listen without judgment, and help connect them to professional support.

If you or someone you know may be in immediate danger or thinking about suicide:
In the U.S., call or text **988** (Suicide & Crisis Lifeline) or text **HOME** to **741741** (Crisis Text Line). If outside the U.S., contact your local emergency number or a local crisis line.

I held my father's hand as he died, and in that same moment, I let go of decades of pain. Death didn't just take him—it took the anger with it. And in its place, it left me with something I never expected: peace.

His urn sits on my mantle next to his favorite gifts I bought him—horses, a symbol of freedom of sorts. I like to think he earned that freedom. After a lifetime of battles, both internal and external, he finally found peace. And in some strange way, so did I.

Sometimes I still catch myself reaching for the phone when I drive past one of his old favorite restaurants. For a split second, my mind forgets he's gone and I think, *I should call Dad, see if he wants that pepper steak tonight.* Then reality sets in, and the silence in the car gets heavier. Grief has a strange way of living with you—it hides in the ordinary moments, in a TV remote, in an empty chair, in the smell of a meal you once shared.

And every time I look at that urn, I whisper the same thing under my breath: *I get it now, Dad. Thank you for letting me love you at the end the way you couldn't at the start.*

Author Reflection Note

If you still have a parent you're at odds with, call them—if you safely can. Visit them. Hear their story before it's too late. Not to excuse what they did, but to understand who they were. Forgiveness doesn't rewrite the past, but it frees your future. I learned that sometimes redemption doesn't come in grand gestures—it comes in holding a trembling hand and choosing to stay when you could have walked away.

We talk a lot about "closure," as if grief were a door that should click shut. But most endings are commas, not periods. The pull toward one last call, one last coffee, one last dance is strong because we ache for an ending we can live with. We want to say the unsaid, to be seen and to see clearly. We want proof that we mattered—and that our story, even the jagged parts, has shape. That final moment isn't about fixing the past. It's about witnessing it: "This is what you gave me. This is what it cost. This is what I'm choosing to carry forward."

Even when the relationship was troubled, we reach for ritual—a hand held in a quiet room, a voicemail saved on a phone, a song played at a wake—because ritual gives weight when words fail. The "last dance" is our way of asking for one true sentence to close the chapter: not to make everything okay, but to keep the best of what was and lay down what we cannot keep carrying.

Sometimes we don't get that moment. The phone goes unanswered. The dance floor never opens. Death interrupts mid-sentence, and we are left with what-ifs. When that happens, grieve the ending you didn't get. Then give yourself the last conversation: write the letter you will never send; speak the words aloud in an empty car; visit the place where the story began; ask a trusted friend to witness what you needed to say. Closure isn't something another person hands us—it's something we practice by telling the truth, setting boundaries, and choosing mercy without abandoning ourselves.

If reconciliation is possible, let it be simple and human. If staying wasn't safe, know that walking away was also an act of love—for yourself and for those who come after you. Either way, let your "last dance" be the way you live now: clearer, kinder, braver.

Anthony James Hodel

Chapter 12:
BMW on Bando Lane

Sobriety, fatherhood, and the climb to becoming a better man.

This was my adult rock bottom.

I violated a probation order for child support—not because I didn't care about my kids, but because I was done feeding the greed. I'd already handed over close to a million dollars in the divorce, only to watch her burn through it in four years on everything but my daughter. When she wanted more, I had nothing left to give.

Financially, I was drowning. Emotionally, I was buried. I had remarried, but the pressure of failure—of feeling trapped and powerless—lit the fuse of my old addiction. The sex addiction came roaring back. I couldn't afford the high-end women anymore, so I descended deeper, chasing the same hollow escape in places that mirrored my own fall—drug-addicted women, broken souls clinging to what was left of themselves.

That's how I ended up at an abandoned house. It was supposed to be a quick escape, just another bad decision in a string of them. Instead, it became my arrest scene. The house was surrounded by police with guns drawn. My BMW stuck out like a sore thumb on "Bando Lane"—clean, polished, and completely out of place. I walked out wearing business attire, trying to hold my composure, the perfect picture of denial, while a redheaded crack addict stumbled behind me.

Someone had called the police to report "two white individuals" walking into the property. I tried to play it off, knowing I had a warrant. I told the officers I was looking at the property as an investment flip and that the woman was just passed out on the sofa. But she told them everything. The act was over. The lies collapsed. Off to jail I went, warrant and all.

And here's the thing: I actually felt a strange sense of relief. The two-year burden I'd been carrying finally lifted. I knew how the courts had treated me for more than fourteen years, and deep down, I knew this was the end of running. I was going to jail.

My attorney—who'd been with me for over twenty years—visited me. He said, "Get in front of this. Tell your wife the truth." But I didn't. I wasn't ready to face her or rub my shame in her face. My story was viable, but she was an auditor—someone who asks questions when she already knows the answers just to see if you're lying. To this day, it's still hard. She continues to stand by me even though, if I were her, I wouldn't be with me.

For a while, I wanted to leave this entire episode out of the book. But one night at a bar with my wife—a few people decided to talk to me out of my name and discuss private details about my issues and my relationship with my wife. That's when I knew she had run around town venting about my actions.

That night, I wasn't drinking. I tried to remain calm. I told one of the guys, "You don't know me well enough to talk to me like this." But he kept going, pushing buttons, trying to provoke something I had buried deep. I warned him again, "Get away from me." He didn't listen. He reached out, trying to grab me—maybe to tackle me or embarrass me in front of the crowd.

Even as an older, out-of-shape 50-year-old, I'm still a former athlete. The switch flipped. "Big mistake," I said out loud. Instinct took over. I picked him up, turned him upside down, and drove him headfirst into the bar chairs.

For a split second, it was like I was seventeen again—the same surge of adrenaline, the same blind reaction that got me expelled years ago. It was déjà vu wrapped in regret. The owner of the bar rushed over, trying to defuse the chaos, and I reacted out of pure instinct, shoving him back. He wasn't my enemy; he was just trying to stop things from getting worse. The 25-year-old kid lay twisted across barstools, stunned and silent.

The police station is literally behind that bar plaza, and they came quick. I told them exactly what happened—that I hadn't been drinking, that I tried to walk away, that I just defended myself when pushed. They could've hauled me in, but they didn't. They gave me a break, and I took it. I called an Uber and went home.

The next morning, I woke up exhausted, emotionally and physically drained. My hands were sore, my head pounding, but my conscience was louder than the pain. I realized something I'd never fully understood before: anger is expensive real estate—it doesn't deserve a single square inch of space in your mind or your soul.

Therapy works. I moved on. To this day, I've never let myself get that angry again. I learned to read the room, to walk away, to feel the storm before it hits. Sometimes growth isn't seen in the moments you explode—it's in the moments you don't.

The moral of the story? You're going to fail over and over. Don't stop trying. The real battle isn't against the court, the addiction, or even the people who hurt you. The real battle is facing yourself and deciding that you deserve better—and then doing better—not for anyone else, but for you.

A Psychologist's Perspective: The Anatomy of Hitting Bottom

From a clinical standpoint, what you just read isn't simply a man falling apart—it's a man confronting the full collapse of denial. In psychology, that moment is called ego disintegration, when the identity we've constructed to protect ourselves finally crumbles under truth.

Addiction—whether sexual, emotional, or chemical—often begins as a coping mechanism for unresolved trauma. It's not about pleasure at its core; it's about anesthesia. The thrill, the chaos, the dopamine—those are just the distractions that keep the pain muted. But the body and brain can't sustain lies forever. Sooner or later, the truth breaks through in the form of loss: loss of freedom, trust, or identity.

When someone hits what's called "rock bottom," the outside world sees destruction. The inside world, however, is often experiencing its first taste of honesty. That's the paradox of redemption—you must lose everything false before you can build anything real.

A psychologist would describe this stage as the beginning of cognitive restructuring—the rewiring of thought patterns that once justified destructive choices. It's when self-awareness replaces self-deception. In therapy, this process often begins with the hardest question of all: "What are you running from?"

In my case, this story reflects a man who had built his worth around control—financial control, romantic control, emotional control. When that structure collapsed, so did the illusion. But it's precisely at that breaking point that transformation begins. Recovery isn't just about abstaining from destructive behavior; it's about replacing those impulses with meaning.

Every addict's brain has a default narrative: "I'm not enough." The work of healing is rewriting that sentence. Not with ego, but with truth. With action. With accountability.

The psychological lesson here is universal: rock bottom isn't the end of your story—it's the end of your denial.

Self-Help Reflection: Facing Your Worst Days

You can't outrun rock bottom.

You can drink, chase, lie, hide, blame—but it'll find you. The key is to stop running and face it head-on. That's the stairway to redemption.

Here's what I learned when I finally stopped lying to myself:

1. **Name Your Hell.**

    Don't sugarcoat it. Write it down. Speak it out loud. Say what you did, what you've become, and what you're afraid of. The only way to reclaim power from your demons is to call them by name. Shame thrives in silence; truth kills it.

2. **Accept the Crash.**

    Stop pretending you can fix it in a day. Healing is brutal. It doesn't come from denial; it comes from acceptance. When you hit your worst day, remind yourself: this is the starting line, not the finish.

3. **Own Your Choices.**

    Don't romanticize your pain. You made decisions—some terrible ones—and that's okay. You can't rewrite yesterday, but you can control tomorrow. Accountability is the currency of self-respect.

4. **Get Uncomfortable with Honesty.**

   You can't rebuild on lies. Tell the truth, even when it rips you apart. Tell your spouse, your therapist, your mentor—someone who will hold you accountable. You can't heal in hiding.

5. **Build the Stairway, One Step at a Time.**

   Redemption isn't one leap—it's daily work. One act of honesty. One apology. One boundary kept. One temptation resisted. One small step that says, I'm not who I was yesterday.

6. **Forgive Yourself, Eventually.**

   You won't feel like you deserve it at first. That's okay. Forgiveness isn't approval—it's permission to stop living in your own prison. It's not saying "I'm fine with what happened." It's saying, "I'm ready to grow from it."

When I got out, I didn't come home a hero. I came home humbled.

The silence after jail is deafening. No one's calling, no one's checking in, and the world just keeps moving without you. You think people will notice when you fall—they don't. You have to learn to climb without applause.

I had to rebuild from the ashes—not just my finances, but my integrity. My word had become a broken promise. Sobriety wasn't a program for me; it was survival. I had to detox from chaos, from adrenaline, from that constant need for validation that had driven every bad decision in my adult life.

Every morning, I woke up and faced the same man in the mirror—the one I had lied to the most. Sobriety wasn't about avoiding alcohol or women. It was about avoiding the mindset that told me I needed either of them to feel alive.

Fatherhood: The Real Reckoning

The hardest part of rebuilding wasn't staying clean—it was showing up for my kids.

They didn't care about my excuses. They didn't want explanations; they wanted consistency. They wanted a dad, not a ghost with good intentions.

There were times I'd sit in my car before seeing them and just cry. I didn't know if I was capable of being what they needed. I was terrified of failing again. But I realized something powerful—kids don't need perfection; they need presence. They need to see you try even after life's beatings.

I started showing up, even when I was tired, broke, or broken. I didn't have fancy gifts, but I had time. And time, when given with intention, can heal what money destroys.

It took years for the walls to come down. My kids didn't trust easily—and I didn't blame them. Every time I wanted to give up, I reminded myself that fatherhood is the truest test of redemption. You can fake smiles, fake business success, fake repentance—but you can't fake love to a child who remembers your absence.

Sobriety: A Stairway, not a Switch

Sobriety wasn't a miracle moment—it was a grind.

There's this lie people love to tell: that one big awakening fixes everything. That's bullshit. It's the small, quiet choices every day that build a new life. Saying "no" when it would be easier to escape.

Walking away from old circles. Admitting when you're triggered instead of pretending you're fine.

At first, it felt lonely. I missed the chaos. The late nights, the rush, the fast life—it all had a gravitational pull. But then, something shifted. I started to feel again. Real emotion. Real gratitude. Real peace.

Sobriety didn't make my life easier—it made it clearer. And when you can finally see yourself clearly, you realize that the pain was always meant to break the shell, not the soul.

Trust: The Long Road Back

Rebuilding trust was the hardest climb on the stairway. My wife didn't owe me forgiveness, and she damn sure didn't owe me a second chance. But she stayed—not because I deserved it, but because she saw something in me that I hadn't yet seen in myself: potential redemption.

Trust isn't rebuilt with words—it's rebuilt with patterns.

It's in showing up when you say you will.

It's in doing what's right when no one's watching.

It's in learning to love without control.

There were nights when I'd catch her watching me, not with affection, but with caution. I had earned that look. But over time, it began to fade, little by little, replaced by something else—respect.

She still challenges me. She still tests me. And honestly, I'm grateful. Because when you've burned down your own house, accountability becomes the new foundation.

Closing Reflection: The Climb Never Ends

Redemption isn't a destination—it's maintenance.

It's brushing your teeth every morning so the decay doesn't return. It's waking up and saying, "I choose to be better today," even when the old voice whispers that you're not worth it.

There's no finish line on the stairway—only higher ground.
Each step is a reminder that your story isn't over.
I used to walk into abandoned houses chasing my next escape.
Now, I walk into my own home, sober, grounded, and proud of the man who finally came back from the dead.

I'm not perfect. I never will be.

But I'm climbing—one step, one day, one choice at a time.
That's redemption.

Anthony James Hodel

Chapter 13:

Anger

"The fire that fueled me — and almost burned me alive."

They say thirteen is a cursed number—a symbol of bad luck. The irony that it landed naturally in this book is not lost on me. Of all the demons I've wrestled, none has lived rent-free in my mind longer than anger. Not the drugs. Not the depression. Not even the trauma. Anger was my most loyal—and most dangerous—companion.

Addiction has triggers. You can trace it back to a moment, a stressor, a craving. For me, the release came in the form of a workout, sex, or even the numb comfort of self-gratification. That pattern had been there since I was twelve. But anger? That was different. That was primal.

Since I was eight years old, I fought daily—sometimes literally. If you looked at me wrong, I swung. I hit teachers, other students, anyone who dared cross my invisible tripwire. It wasn't about winning—it was about unloading the fire I didn't know how to carry.

My childhood, teenage years, and adulthood all carried the same theme—violence at the drop of a hat. I punched holes in walls, smashed windshields, even ripped the mirror off a brand-new Escalade in a fit of rage. If I was drinking, it was worse—domestic violence, screaming matches, full-blown explosions. Alcohol was just gasoline poured on an already raging fire. It was in my DNA, hardcoded into me, and when you throw liquor on top of that, it turned me into a complete asshole and a reckless one at that.

Every legal problem, every fight I'd ever been in seemed to have one thing in common—they happened when I was intoxicated. I didn't even drink daily—just a few days a week—but those nights always came with a price. A $300 tab, five to ten martinis or IPAs, and three days of recovery. Misery loves company, they say. And anger? Anger loves the energy booze gives it, letting it run rampant until nothing and no one is safe.

Fast-forward to fifty-two years old, and I can tell you without hesitation: nothing ever controlled me more than anger.

"For 90 days, I planned a murder."

I could taste the violence. Feel the weight of the gun. I was ready to trade my life for revenge.

But here's the thing— When rage owns you, your enemy has already won.

I had to choose: Feed the fire until it turned me to ash or put it out and rebuild from nothing.

I chose to rebuild.

The Breaking Point

I realized how bad it had gotten when I spent ninety straight days plotting how I would kill my ex-wife. She had drained me financially, weaponized my daughter against me, called the FBI, the Attorney General—playing the scorned woman role while I was working fully within the law. One million dollars gone, and I still owed child support every month.

Then came the tabloid article. Then the online comments. Then the constant chase for more money. I snapped. I didn't want to "get even." I wanted blood. I had the plan down to the sickest, most precise detail—shoot her in the legs first so she would feel it. Then tell her exactly why she was dying. Then the stomach, the chest, and finally, the head.

That is how far gone I was. I was ready to trade the rest of my life for a cell—or turn the gun on myself after. And here's the messed-up truth: all the trauma I'd lived through didn't hit me the way this did. This was the woman I had built a family with, and that betrayal landed differently.

I'll talk more about relationships later, and how I own my part in the collapse of them, but right now this is about rage—the kind that doesn't just visit, it moves in and redecorates the place.

The Moment I Stepped Back

I absorbed lawsuit after lawsuit, bad media coverage while she cashed the monthly checks. And here's what I can tell you: when you're that consumed, the person you're aiming at already won. They control your mind, your body, your soul.

One morning, I woke up and told my current wife, "I have to get help. I can't live like this." I told her the truth—my violent fantasy, my obsession with it. She didn't run. She didn't flinch. She just listened.

I signed up for seventeen weeks of therapy. I went in expecting homework assignments, self-help books, little exercises to "take the edge off." But I knew within the first few sessions: I was either going to be all in, or I was going to coast for a few weeks and slide back into the old me.

I chose all in.

A Psychologist's Perspective: Understanding the Fire Within

During my time in college, I took psychology courses that opened my eyes to what was really happening inside my mind. Later, through therapy, those lessons became personal. A psychologist once explained it to me like this:

"Anger isn't the root emotion—it's the guard dog. It protects what's underneath: fear, shame, hurt, and loss of control."

That sentence hit me harder than any punch I'd thrown.

From a clinical standpoint, anger is a secondary emotion—a mask for deeper pain. When trauma occurs early in life, especially for children who grow up in chaos or abuse, the nervous system learns to live in "fight or flight" mode. Over time, that state becomes your default programming. It's not just emotional—it's biological.

In my case, anger was my nervous system doing what it was trained to do: defend, attack, survive. Every confrontation triggered a chemical storm—adrenaline, cortisol, and dopamine—that felt addictive. That's why so many people who've experienced trauma confuse anger for strength. It feels powerful. It gives the illusion of control.

But psychologists will tell you the truth: chronic anger erodes the brain's ability to regulate emotion, distorts judgment, and rewires memory around threat. It makes the world feel dangerous—even when it's not. It's not weakness; it's conditioning.

That's why therapy mattered. Cognitive-behavioral therapy (CBT) helped me rewire my triggers. Instead of reacting instantly, I learned to name what I was actually feeling—hurt, fear, rejection—and let that be okay. Over time, my brain learned something revolutionary: I could feel without having to fight.

That's the real lesson I carried from college psychology into adulthood—understanding the mechanics of anger doesn't erase it, but it gives you the tools to control it before it controls you.

The Shift

The person I was consumed with destroying is still out there. Still unhappy. Still running the same script. And I now understand why—because unless you do your own inventory, unless you dig into your own wreckage, you'll never find peace. Based on her makeup, I'm willing to bet she's got her own unhealed trauma.

Me? I'm living a relatively happy life now. Not perfect—life never is—but manageable. Challenges still show up at my door, but now I have tools to deal with them. And those tools have rewired my fight-or-flight response in ways I never thought possible.

Self-Help Action Plan: Managing the Fire Before It Burns You

Name It Out Loud – You can't control what you won't admit. Say "I'm angry" without sugarcoating it.

Get Distance – Physical and mental space can be the difference between making a point and making a prison sentence.

Identify the Trigger – Stress? Betrayal? Disrespect? Knowing your trigger is the first step to disarming it.

Channel It into Motion – Lift weights, run, hit a heavy bag, scream into a pillow. Move it out of your body.

Therapy is a Tool, not a Punishment – Commit to the work. Half-effort equals half-results.

Separate Person from Pattern – Often, the person making you furious is operating from their own unresolved wounds.

Decide Who Controls You – Every second you let anger own your thoughts, you've given your opponent the win.

Advice I Learned the Hard Way

One of the most powerful lessons I've learned came while watching my father pass and endure suffering. It made me realize how precious time truly is.

I've always been competitive, driven to work day and night, but here's the truth: you can't take the money with you. At the end of the day, time is all we really have—and the next minute is never guaranteed.

So I've made the decision to step back, enjoy more free time, and create memories that matter. Travel, fine dining, sporting events, plays, and experiences with people I love—that's what makes life full.

My advice to anyone reading this: don't wait until life forces you to slow down to start living. Success isn't just about the grind; it's about enjoying the rewards along the way.

Closing Reflection

Anger stole enough of my years. It ruined relationships, cost me peace, and nearly cost me my freedom. Today, I understand that the same fire that once burned everything down can also light the path forward—if you learn how to control it.

I've spent half my life reacting, and the other half learning how not to. The lesson? Rage may have built my armor, but peace became my strength.

The day you learn to master your anger, you don't just win—you become untouchable.

Anger Incidents I Can't Forget

We talk about anger like it's an attitude problem. Mine was a demolition crew. I've had more blowouts than I can count, but a few are burned into me.

The first was in my twenties with my first wife. We'd been day-drinking and ended up at a Denny's after midnight. She started in on me and I fired back—loud, public, ugly. A security guard stepped in. I shoved him into a counter and told her, 'We have to go.' She refused. She walked home—in a skirt and heels—in a winter storm. I sped off in my dealer demo, a new Cadillac, running lights and flying down side streets. Police lit me up. I pulled into my apartment complex, bailed from the car, and ran. Back then, I had track speed. They brought out dogs. They found me. Fleeing, pursuit, and DUI. 1997. Next day, top attorney. The paper called me 'the running man.'

Years later, we were in a limo when a fight exploded—bottles flying, bodies everywhere. The driver pulled over; police swarmed the car. I started swinging at cops. I woke up in jail, no bond, psych eval ordered. Stacked charges with double-digit time possible. Attorney, counseling, and monitoring conditions kept me out of prison; they didn't fix my soul.

With my current wife: argument spilled into the men's room. I turned and threw a punch not knowing it was her. Horror hit mid-swing. I fled, vaulted a rail, and dropped fifteen feet through trees. Same attorney, same mitigation dance.

These reels still play. That's why I don't drink, why I work my recovery. Today, no booze, no blow-ups. Peace is cheaper than bail.

Car Lot at Midnight — Gun in My Ribs

At my angriest, I was running hot on steroids, pride, and a taste for fast wins. Got hired at a car lot in my twenties working for a man named John—today he's a close friend I talk to almost every day. What I didn't know when I walked in was that his childhood looked a lot like mine: rough edges, hard knocks, no guarantees. What connected us wasn't just hustle—it was that he'd figured it out. John was a self-made millionaire who refused to stay a product of where he started.

I came in young and hungry and turned that store into a well-oiled machine. We were printing money and, before long, John and I were expanding into other ventures together. Success became adrenaline. Adrenaline became identity.

One night, closing the store, the lot was quiet—late, dark, and not the nicest neighborhood. I had my back turned when a man pressed a gun into my side. Without thinking, I said, "You're not taking my stuff that easy. Shoot me—you'd be doing me a favor." That wasn't courage. That was a cocktail of anger, greed, and steroids talking. Looking back, that line could've ended my life on the asphalt. I didn't care about tomorrow; I only cared about not being small today. That's what rage does: it makes death feel like a bargain if it means you don't feel powerless for one more second.

College — Dialed Up and Dangerous

Rewind to college. I walked around dialed up and always on edge—steroids in my system, anger in my veins. At football camp, the so-called All-American linebacker wouldn't stop talking crazy. First live rep, I hit him so hard I knocked him out of bounds in practice. I stood over him and said, "You ain't shit." From that day on, he ran his mouth every chance he got.

One night in the frat dorms he popped off again. He was the resident assistant; I was the problem the RA manual doesn't cover. I blasted him in the mouth. The next day I was suspended from campus and the team—sent home on leave until peer court and the university president met about me. A professor stepped in and let me stay at his house while it was all sorted out. If I hadn't been an athlete, I probably would've been gone for good. Football saved my life by giving my rage somewhere legal to go—even if it almost lost me the chance to stay in school.

Anthony James Hodel

Chapter 14:

The 44 Foundation

Turning Pain into Purpose, One Life at a Time

*"The 44 Foundation wasn't born from wealth—
it was born from wounds that refused to waste their pain."*
— Anthony J. Hodel

When I hit my 50s, something inside me shifted. I stopped looking in the mirror to check how I looked and started looking to ask who I'd become.

For decades, I'd let anger control me. I bought houses with more square footage than I needed, cars that could've paid for a kid's college tuition, suits tailored down to the millimeter. I told myself it was the reward for hard work—but deep down, I knew it was camouflage.

Every material thing was another brick in the wall I built to hide the pain. The trauma. The guilt. The fear. The little boy inside me who still wanted to be seen, to be loved, to matter.

But the thing about pain is that it doesn't disappear when you bury it under success. It festers. It finds new ways to leak out—through anger, addiction, or isolation.

I spent years dancing with evil. I thought I was celebrating success, but really, I was feeding my demons. Every bottle popped, every check written, every deal closed was another spin on that dance floor.

Then one day, I stopped dancing.

I remember walking through one of my own houses—marble floors, chandeliers, custom artwork—and feeling absolutely empty. Everything I thought mattered didn't. Every possession was just another reflection of how lost I really was.

I started asking harder questions: What if I used the same energy I used to destroy myself to build something greater than me? What if the pain was the point? What if God didn't curse me with it—but trusted me with it?

That's when the cliché hit home: God gives the hardest battles to His strongest soldiers.

I used to hate hearing that. I'd think, "Then why the hell me?" But now, I understand. I was selected because I could handle it—and because I could help others handle it too.

The idea for The 44 Foundation came during one of the quietest seasons of my life. No champagne. No chaos. Just stillness.

I thought about my father—his flaws, his pain, and his name. For years, I ran from that name because of the chaos tied to it. But over time, I realized running wasn't redemption. Building was.

The 44 Foundation is more than a foundation. It's a resurrection. A second chance for the Hodel name. A chance to redirect the same energy that nearly destroyed me into something that heals others.

I built it small—humble beginnings. A few donations here, a sponsorship there. But it's not about scale; it's about soul. Every step forward feels like another brick laid on the road to recovery—not just for me, but for my family's legacy.

One day, when people hear the name Hodel, I don't want them to think of the chaos or the addiction. I want them to think of impact, empathy, and integrity.

That's what The 44 Foundation is meant to do—divert my demons into something divine.

In my 20s and 30s, buying things made me feel alive. In my 50s, giving things makes me feel human.

I started giving back—to people, to animals, to causes that resonated with my story. I began to understand that fulfillment doesn't come from what you own, but from what you offer.

Each act of giving became medicine. It silenced the noise in my head and replaced it with meaning.

St. Jude's Children's Research Hospital taught me that real courage comes in the smallest bodies. Those kids fight like warriors while most adults crumble under far less.

ASPCA reminded me that love doesn't have a voice—it has eyes that look at you and say "thank you" without words. Animals, like children, don't choose their circumstances.

Wounded Warrior Project made me realize that some heroes never stop fighting, even after the war ends. They carry invisible wounds that need more than medals—they need community.

Susan G. Komen Foundation reminded me that cancer doesn't just affect one—it ripples through families, testing love and faith at every turn.

Cleveland Playhouse Donor's Circle connected me to creativity, expression, and healing through art—the same kind of performance and emotion that saved me countless times from breaking.

And through Athletic Scholarship Corporation, I began donating recruiting services to inner-city youth, giving them a shot at college exposure and the mentorship I wish I'd had. These kids are one "yes" away from rewriting their entire future.

Each of these causes became a thread in The 44 Foundation's fabric—woven together by empathy and experience.

The truth is, every time I help someone else heal, I heal a little too. It's almost spiritual—the way giving rewires pain into purpose.

When I meet a family at St. Jude's or a veteran at a fundraiser, I don't see charity—I see connection. I see the reflection of every broken part of me that finally found light.

The 44 Foundation started small—humble, almost invisible. But I've learned that the most powerful movements often begin that way.

My vision is to expand it into scholarships, youth mentorship, animal rescue initiatives, and philanthropic programs that will outlive me. My demons may have fueled destruction once—but now they fuel redemption.

For generations, our family name was tied to dysfunction, addiction, and pain. My mission is to rewrite that history—not erase it, but transform it.

The 44 Foundation is my way of saying to the next Hodel who carries this name: "You come from fire—but you were born to light, not burn."

One day, I want my children and grandchildren to walk into a hospital wing, an animal shelter, or a youth training facility and see our name on the wall—not because of what we took, but because of what we gave.

That's redemption. That's legacy. That's how you turn a curse into a crown.

A Psychologist's Perspective: Healing Through Purpose

When I was in college, I remember sitting in a behavioral psychology class where the professor said, "Purpose is the most effective antidepressant known to man."

That line hit me years later when I began my own healing. I came to understand, both personally and through my studies, that human beings crave significance. We are wired to matter.

Psychologists call it post-traumatic growth—the phenomenon where survivors of trauma don't just recover, they rebuild stronger. They find new meaning, deeper empathy, and an appreciation for life they never had before.

What I learned in those college classrooms was that pain, when left untreated, becomes poison. But pain that's understood, processed, and redirected can become power.

The foundation became my therapy. Each donation, each mentorship, each project was a living demonstration of behavioral recovery in motion. Cognitive-behavioral principles teach that changing your behavior—even before you feel ready—can alter your emotional state. That's exactly what happened. I gave first, and the healing followed.

My professors would say that purpose is the bridge between trauma and transformation. I never forgot that. Giving back doesn't just fix the world—it fixes the giver.

That's why The 44 Foundation isn't simply a charity. It's an emotional laboratory. A space where pain transforms into service, and service transforms into peace.

The psychologist in me understands it scientifically; the survivor in me understands it spiritually. Together, they remind me that the best way to heal from your story is to use it to rewrite someone else's.

You don't need a foundation or a trust fund to make an impact. Here's how to start right where you are:

1. Turn your pain into a project. Take the thing that nearly destroyed you and make it your mission to protect others from it.
2. Start small but stay consistent. Don't wait to be rich to be generous. Consistency builds credibility—and credibility builds change.
3. Give your time, not just your wallet. Money helps, but presence heals. Show up. Volunteer. Listen.
4. Involve your family. Let your kids see you giving. Teach them that success without service is failure in disguise.
5. Measure impact, not applause. The loudest acts aren't always the most meaningful. Quiet generosity creates louder echoes over time.
6. Heal forward. Use giving as therapy. Every person you help is another step away from who you used to be.

I once thought I needed to save the world. Now I realize I just need to save one life at a time.

Maybe that's a child who gets a scholarship. Maybe it's a veteran who finds peace. Maybe it's an abused animal who finally feels safe. Or maybe—it's me.

Because every time I give, I take one step closer to freedom. The 44 Foundation isn't just about money. It's about meaning.

It's my way of telling the world that the boy who once lived in chaos learned to build calm. That the man who once broke things learned to build trust—literally and symbolically.

When I'm gone, I don't want people to talk about what I had. I want them to talk about who I helped.

The 44 Foundation is my promise—to myself, my family, and the world—that darkness doesn't get the final word. Pain may have written the early chapters of my life, but purpose will finish the book.

To anyone reading this, hear me clearly: You don't need to be perfect to give back. You just need to be willing.

Start small. Start today. Because legacy doesn't begin when you die—it begins when you decide to live for something bigger than yourself.

That's what The 44 Foundation stands for. That's what redemption looks like.

Anthony James Hodel

Chapter 15:
The Distance That Raised Me

How Missing My Children Broke Me Open

"Love is not what you feel on birthdays; it's what you do on Tuesdays—when the school calls, when the cop lights flash, when your chest is tight and you show up anyway."

I didn't plan on three kids with three different women. Pain finds pain if neither of you has learned to hold it without bleeding. This is about missing my children—across rooms and years—and how that missing taught me more than winning ever did.

The shape of the ache (and what the data says).

There's a particular silence in a house where a child should be. It hums under the fridge and behind the blinds. In the United States, that silence is not rare: in 2018 about 26.5% of children under 21 lived in a home where one parent lived elsewhere. Most of the time the resident parent is the mother—about four in five custodial parents (79.9%)—which means the nonresident parent is usually the father. A national review of 2018 data estimates roughly three out of four nonresident parents are fathers. These facts don't make the ache noble; they make it common.

Fathers are not optional extras. Decades of research link father involvement to better outcomes for kids—school, behavior, health. But fathers who live apart from their children participate less frequently in day-to-day care than dads under the same roof; the gap shows up in national surveys that track how often dads talk, read, help with homework, or ferry kids to activities. The more we're pushed to the perimeter, the harder it is to stay in the game.

What makes contact so hard?

Some barriers are logistical and brutal: distance after a breakup, money, and work schedules. Large studies of separated families keep circling back to the same trio—repartnering, relocation, and residual conflict—as the big forces that drag father-child contact down over time. Mothers and fathers also perceive those lows differently: in qualitative work, mothers often report fathers "aren't interested," while fathers say they're being cut out. Both can be true in different homes.

Some barriers are structural. In England and Wales, for example, private-law child-arrangements cases (the ones about where children live and how they see each parent) take close to a year on average to reach a final order—around 42 weeks across 2024, improving to about 39 weeks in spring 2025 but still far from quick. Delays like that turn months into missed birthdays.

Some barriers are behavioral. Researchers use terms like "maternal gatekeeping" (when the resident parent limits or shapes the other parent's involvement) and parental alienating behaviors (PABs), behaviors intended to damage a child's relationship with the other parent. In a U.S.–Canada poll-based, peer-reviewed study, 35.5% of U.S. parents who had children reported being targets of alienating behaviors; about 13.7% said they were currently restricted from seeing one or more children. Among those who said they were targeted, two-thirds believed the behaviors led to a child being alienated from them. Self-reports aren't the same as court findings, but they map the lived experience many fathers describe.

And we need a clear-eyed caveat: sometimes contact is limited for safety. After separations involving intimate partner violence, limiting or supervising contact can be necessary to protect a child (and the other parent). One truth does not cancel the other.

How often "no contact" really happens.

If you zoom out, you see mixed pictures by country—but the pattern is consistent: most separated children do see their nonresident parent, and a meaningful minority do not.

- Australia: In court-ordered arrangements, no-contact orders are rare (≈3%). In the general separated population, about 9% of arrangements involve no contact with fathers.

- United Kingdom: Government tracking (Understanding Society) reports 56% of children in separated families saw the nonresident parent at least fortnightly in 2021–22—which implies the rest saw that parent less often or not at all. A 2022 literature review for the Children's Commissioner cites estimates that about 13% of nonresident fathers had no contact.

- United States: Hard national counts of why contact fails are scarce, but the landscape offers clues. In 2018 CPS–Child Support data, among families with child-support arrangements, about half of noncustodial parents had visitation privileges without shared custody, 30.6% had some joint custody, and 19.4% had neither joint custody nor visitation written into the order—an administrative picture of how many cases proceed without formalized parenting time. Because ~80% of custodial parents are mothers, these "no-visitation-in-the-order" cases often involve fathers. (Orders are not the same as actual contact, but orders shape it.)

When love gets used as leverage

I have known the weaponized version of this story—the missed hand-offs, the sudden "the child is sick" texts that always land ten minutes before pick-up, the slow poisoning of my name in the child's ear. The literature has names for parts of that: restrictive gatekeeping (limits, undermining, inflexible rules) and alienating behaviors (disparagement, blocking contact, false narratives). Studies show these behaviors are associated with lower father involvement and worse co-parenting quality. They don't only come from mothers—but since mothers are more often the resident parent, the gate often sits at their door.

At the same time, the numbers warn against turning every locked door into a villain. Some parents limit contact because they fear for safety or doubt the other parent's capacity or sobriety; courts see that every day. And sometimes fathers fall off—crushed by cost, distance, shame, or a new family. The data tells both stories.

What the fight costs (and why some keep fighting)?

Time, money, and faith. In the UK, a final order can take roughly 9–10 months; in many places in the U.S., enforcing a parenting plan means motion practice and contempt—a process that can be slow and expensive, especially unrepresented. Those are months and dollars dads can't get back. And still—many show up anyway.

Because when contact does happen, kids benefit. Even the cautious government data says it: fathers' presence and participation correlate with better outcomes. That's the quiet miracle of everyday fatherhood—geometry homework at the kitchen table, a sideline on a windy Saturday, a voice in the dark saying "I'm here."

What my missing taught me

I learned to document, not detonate—to save the messages, keep my language clean, and ask the court for time, not vengeance. I learned that flexibility beats fury when a child gets sick or a shift runs late. And I learned that kids measure love in hours, not arguments. The system moves; sometimes it crawls. The other parent moves; sometimes they close the door. My job is to keep showing up at the hinge.

And if you need the headline numbers that sit behind the feeling:

- Most separated kids still see their nonresident parent, but a non-trivial minority don't (≈9–13% in high-quality snapshots overseas; U.S. administrative data show many cases with no visitation written into orders).

- Fathers are usually the nonresident parent (≈75%), because mothers are usually the custodial parent (~80%).

- Alienating behaviors are reported by a sizable share of parents, and a notable share say they're currently restricted from seeing their kids—real signals that, in some families, access is being used as leverage.

None of that proves who is right in any given home. It just proves the ache wasn't in my head. And on the Tuesdays when it would have been easier to go numb, that ache kept me moving—toward the next pick-up, the next school call, the next small chance to be a father.

Savannah — The First Lesson

Savannah made me a father. I was a great dad and a terrible husband—anger raging, addiction peaking. Still, I clocked in without a time clock: baths, bottles, diapers, midnight rocking, five a.m. feedings.

Money looked like stability but wasn't. Depression spoke quietly in that house while my pain yelled. Early years, I saw her often; later, money and control poisoned every handoff.

I documented, I called first when I knew police were coming, and I refused to fold when seven cruisers lined my street. A sergeant who once played football with me cleared the scene. We got a few quiet weeks—normal out of rubble.

We later took emergency custody. Structure met rebellion. I asked the court for help because I feared where it was going. She's grown now. I haven't heard her voice in almost nine years.

Peyton — When Denial Met the Truth

We were engaged. I was looping the same self-destruction. One week in D.C., dinner with the President, stress like rebar in my chest. Then I saw her face on an escort site. Denials. Proof. Detonation.

She was pregnant. I said he wasn't mine. Fifteen years later, DNA said otherwise. When he was little, we were tight. Then Florida, then a decade of withholding. I paid support for a child I couldn't see.

I finally pushed for DNA in court. Missed dates for her brought no warrant; one miss for me meant cuffs. Counseling followed. He has a right to be angry. I should have fought earlier. Avoidance is its own violence.

Jedidiah — The One I Tried to Do Right

I met his mother online. I tried to set aside the chaos and build something real. I walked into a life already on fire—losing a home, multiple kids, pressure from every direction. Words said stability; actions said chaos.

She said she was pregnant. I demanded DNA for years. Around three years old, the papers came; the test said he's mine. I got rights, but withholding continued. Therapists wouldn't step in without her consent. Sessions got sabotaged.

Truth: my wife of ten years has never met my sons. Sometimes I call that peace. Sometimes it's a character flaw. The kids deserved the best of me, not the most exhausted version.

The Real Confession

I could be a good father on camera and a failing one off camera. I brought the war inside the house. I'm learning steadiness, not speeches.

What My Kids Got Right

I know my children—now adults—grew up mad at me and confused. I understand that they should be.

Confusion is honest. Anger is honest. When a parent is absent, the body keeps a tally the mind can't quite balance. You were asked to carry a mystery that wasn't yours. You were asked to explain a father you didn't hire.

This is not a defense. It's a confirmation: **you read the situation correctly.** When I didn't show, you learned that love can be a weather pattern. When I arrived with promises and exit wounds, you learned that belief can be a bruise.

I can't return your childhood. I can't get back my lost time stolen. I can tell you what I've learned about what absence does to a kid and the adult they become. And I can practice steadying the room now, not with speeches but with small, boring, Tuesday choices.

The Physics of Absence (How It Lands in a Child's Body)

Absence isn't empty; it's heavy. Kids fill it with self-blame because self-blame feels like control.

- **If it's my fault, I can fix it.**
- **If I'm better, they'll stay.**
- **If I don't need, I won't be left.**

A child's nervous system learns to scan the door instead of the present moment. That scan becomes a habit: hypervigilance that masquerades as maturity; detachment that masquerades as calm. The house trains the heartbeat.

When the parent returns, the nervous system whiplashes—reaching while bracing, clinging while pushing away. Kids call this "acting out." Adults call it "mixed signals." The body calls it survival.

Early Signs
(What Kids Do When They're Trying to Survive)

- **Perfecting:** Straight-A's as a locksmith. If I'm flawless, they'll choose me.

- **Performing:** Funny, helpful, charismatic—the child who manages everyone's mood.

- **Parentifying:** Becoming the reliable adult too early; learning bills before birthdays.

- **Withdrawing:** Quiet, compliant, "easy." The cost is invisibility.

- **Exploding:** Big feelings with no safe landing strip. The explosion gets them in trouble and proves they're "too much," which confirms the fear underneath.

None of this means the child is broken; it means the environment was demanding. The strategies worked. That's why they're hard to set down.

Grown-Up Echoes
(How Childhood Absence Repeats Itself)

The calendar flips but the body keeps yesterday. Below are the common echoes I see—how absence in childhood can shape adulthood. If you recognize yourself here, you're not dramatic; you're accurate.

1) Confidence

What happens: Confidence becomes conditional. You either outwork everyone to outrun abandonment or you sandbag your gifts so no one can judge your actual best.

How it shows up:

- Impostor moves: downplaying wins, overexplaining, waiting to be "found out."

- Overachieving as anesthesia; rest feels dangerous.

- Self-sabotage right before success—ending it yourself so no one else can.

What helps now:

- **Tiny proofs:** stack five-minute wins (call back, send the email, keep a promise to yourself).

- **Externalize the critic:** give the voice a name; it's not the truth, it's a tape.

- **Borrowed mirror:** let people you trust describe you and don't argue—write it down and reread on bad days.

2) Love & Relationships

What happens: Attachment injuries lean anxious, avoidant, or both. You may test love to see if it holds or starve it to stay safe.

How it shows up:

- **Anxious:** constant checking, overexplaining, protest behaviors ("If you loved me, you'd know").

- **Avoidant:** pulling away when closeness increases; independence used as armor.

- **Disorganized:** wanting and fleeing at the same time; confusing even to yourself.

What helps now:

- **Name your pattern** without villainizing it—"I tend to pursue/withdraw when I'm scared."

- **Pre-agreement:** tell partners how to find you in conflict ("If I go quiet, give me 20 minutes then check back").

- **Repair faster:** it's not "never rupture," it's "rupture, own it, repair."

3) Trust

What happens: Trust becomes a ledger. You need receipts to feel safe because promises were a currency that once bounced.

How it shows up:

- Testing people to make the future predictable—saying "it's fine" then keeping score.
- Scanning for inconsistencies more than you scan for effort.
- Confusing intensity with safety; chaos with chemistry.

What helps now:

- **Pattern view > promise view:** watch what repeats.
- **Trust budget:** set small limits you can afford to lose; expand when patterns hold.
- **Two truths:** you can be cautious *and* open; you can doubt *and* proceed.

4) Decision-Making

What happens: When you grew up waiting for the other shoe, you may either deliberate forever or decide in a sprint to end the tension.

How it shows up:

- Paralysis by analysis—seeking one more opinion, one more scenario.

- Emergency choices—jobs, moves, relationships picked for relief, not alignment.

- Outsourcing choices to authority figures or partners, then resenting them for it.

What helps now:

- **If-then rules:** "If I have 70% data and a next step, I decide by 5 p.m."

- **Body check:** does this choice feel like constriction or expansion?

- **Post-decision ritual:** write why you chose; revisit later to recalibrate, not to punish.

5) Boundaries & Belonging

What happens: Kids of absence learn to earn their place. Saying "no" feels like gambling with love.

How it shows up:

- Overcommitting, under-resourced.

- Fawning—agreeing to avoid conflict, then feeling invisible.

- Hyper-independence: refusing help because needing has been dangerous.

What helps now:

- **Boundaries as direction, not defense:** "Here's what I will/won't do," not "Here's what you must do."

- **Ask small:** accept help on micro-tasks to retrain the nervous system.

- **Belonging test:** if belonging requires you to disappear, it's not belonging.

6) Work, Money, and Control

What happens: Money and titles look like stability, so they become personality. Control is love in a language you can speak.

How it shows up:

- Hustle as identity; collapse on weekends.

- Micromanaging because delegation feels like abandonment risk.

- Spending or hoarding to self-soothe, then shame.

What helps now:

- **Security stack:** savings, routines, and relationships that don't depend on performance.

- **Permission to be medium:** pick one area where "good enough" is the new ceiling this month.

- **Let someone help** with one meaningful task; annotate the outcome.

A Note to Savannah, to Peyton, to Jedidiah

You were right to be angry. You were accurate to be confused. I didn't give you the pattern children need: predictability. Love counts most on Tuesdays, and I wasn't there on enough Tuesdays.

I am not asking you to move on. I'm asking you to move **through**—at your pace, with your boundaries. If we talk, I'll answer the question you actually ask. If you need distance, I'll stand far enough back to prove you're not responsible for me.

When you say, "You left," I won't revise the story. When you say, "You came back and made it harder," I won't litigate context. I'll listen. Then I'll ask, "what does repair looks like to you?" And I'll do the boring part: keep doing it after the apology high wears off.

Field Notes from a Psychologist's Lens (Extended)

- **Attachment injuries repair with proximity plus predictability.** Not grand gestures—*predictable*, boring presence over time. (I had to learn boring is holy.)

What I'd Do Differently

Choose peace over being right; steadiness wins.

Build a boring home—predictable dinner, bedtime, tone.

Support without control; no weaponizing money.

Never talk through the child; use neutral tools.

Apologize without a receipt; show, don't sell.

Do the work: therapy, recovery, sleep, movement.

Make Tuesdays sacred—small calls, big trust.

A Psychologist's Lens

Attachment injuries repair with predictable contact and attunement.

High-conflict co-parenting creates loyalty binds; parallel-parenting helps.

Parentification steals childhood; keep adults in the adult lane.

Reunification therapy works when readiness exists; don't force timelines.

Missing my children taught me how to stay—in myself. If you three ever read this: I'm here to remain, to listen, and to make Tuesdays sacred again.

Anthony James Hodel

Chapter 16:
The Redemption Stairway

"Redemption isn't one big leap—it's a thousand honest steps."

You probably purchased this book because there's pain in you that hasn't found a home yet. I get it. I bought every mask money could buy trying to cover mine. If you're holding this chapter and reading these words, you're already on the stairway with me.

Peace, for me, has been an elusive state. I've learned where it hides: in privacy, in self-help, and in helping others. I can't change the past—and whether I would change it now is complicated. I lived a colorful life: loud wins, louder losses, more failures than success. Today my life is calm and mostly basic. I enjoy time with my wife, coffee on the patio, and walking the dog who thinks I'm a world champion just for coming home.

I named this chapter **The Redemption Stairway**. I used that term often because it fits—only it isn't a neat staircase. It's twisty and uneven. You'll miss steps. You'll tumble. You'll go back down three flights just to notice a new handrail you somehow never used. But there *is* a top, and the climb is worth your breath.

Redemption isn't one big leap—it's a thousand honest steps. People expect a grand, cinematic moment of redemption. A man walks out of a courtroom exonerated. A trophy held high under stadium lights. A clean slate and a standing ovation.

But real redemption? It's not an event. It's a daily practice.

It's crying in your car and still driving home without making the call you used to make. It's walking your dog instead of walking back into temptation. It's skipping the drink, the text, the secret you know would unravel everything.

Redemption is quiet. Redemption is messy. Redemption is choosing to show up even when nobody sees you.

At 27, I had the life that magazines sell. Foreign cars. Plush homes. Custom suits. Awards in glass cases. A bank account most people would envy. But inside, I was rotting. I'd pull over on my drive home, chest tight, tears streaming. Look in the mirror and not recognize the man looking back. Ask myself, "How long can you live like this?"

Everyone thought I was cocky, egotistical, bulletproof. But all of that—the cars, the suits, the corner offices—was camouflage for a man who was quietly dying inside. That awareness was my first step. I didn't know it yet, but that was pre-redemption.

I was twelve when my grandfather gave me my first bench press set. Plastic Joe Weider weights filled with sand. I stacked every plate on the bar, bent it, and got one shaky rep. I stood up like I'd benched the world. That wasn't about strength—it was about ownership. A place I could control. A seed of discipline that would become the foundation of my healing.

Later in life, I built businesses and wore the suit of a man in control. But I led a double life. I fed my demons with women and work—flying in high-end companions, spending thousands to escape the emptiness. It wasn't drugs. It wasn't alcohol. But it was addiction.

I placed the burden of healing me onto my wife. I made her pay for things others did to me. There were police calls, a car crash we should've died in. That survival was God's message: This is your last chance.

I upset her family. I broke trust. But her children still love me. That's grace. That's redemption in real time. Everyone gets an angel or two—my grandmother was one. My wife is another.

You can't truly love anyone until you love yourself. Until you face your pain and start owning it. It's not their job to fix you. It's yours.

Celebrate your wins quietly. Not everyone is rooting for you. Tell your dog. He'll listen without judgment.

Redemption is built with repetition. Small honest actions, done daily.

A Typical Stairway to Redemption

For a victim of abuse or an addict, the stairway to redemption isn't glamorous. It's shaky, slow, and full of traps. Here's what it often looks like:

1. **The Basement (Denial):** You numb, hide, and swear you're fine. But fine means "Freaked-out, Insecure, Neurotic, Exhausted."

2. **Step 1 – Admit it Once:** Tell one safe person the truth.

3. **Step 2 – Safety First:** Remove immediate danger—lock the bottle, block the numbers.

4. **Step 3 – Small Routine:** Water. Breathe. Move. Repeat.

5. **Step 4 – Name Your Pattern:** Learn your triggers.

6. **Step 5 – Move the Body:** Heal through movement.

7. **Step 6 – Add People:** Isolation kills progress.

8. **Step 7 – Practice the Pause:** Wait 10 seconds before reacting.

9. **Step 8 – Repair or Release:** Make amends or let go.

10. **Step 9 – Build Meaning:** Serve others. Mentor. Create.

11. **Step 10 – Expect Falls:** Falling isn't failure; it's feedback.

12. **Step 11 – Keep It Boring:** Boring means stable. Stable means healing.

Healing isn't measured by the number of days sober or the pages of a journal—it's measured by how quickly you get up after you fall.

The Reality of Recovery

According to national studies, recovery takes time. The median number of serious attempts is **two**, though many take five or more. On average, it takes **four to five years** of sustained effort for risk levels to drop close to normal. Relapse rates hover around **40–60%**, similar to conditions like hypertension. The point: relapse doesn't mean failure—it means you're still fighting.

Many of us fail before we succeed. On average, someone may relapse multiple times before permanent recovery. But the truth? **Every single attempt counts.** Every effort rewires your brain. Every small victory strengthens your resolve.

Addiction and trauma go hand in hand. The abused child becomes the adult chasing chaos because peace feels foreign. Healing means re-teaching yourself to sit in stillness without panic.

Building Your Plan

Create a one-page redemption plan. Keep it simple.

1. Daily Non-Negotiables

- Wake up early. Drink water. Move your body.

- Talk to someone you trust.

- Do one kind thing daily.

2. Identify Triggers
Know what sets you off—boredom, rejection, stress, loneliness.

3. Interrupt the Pattern
Take ten deep breaths. Walk. Pray. Text your support person.

4. Surround Yourself with Accountability
Keep two or three people who will tell you the truth. They don't need to fix you—they just need to see you.

5. Service and Purpose
Nothing replaces helping others. When you pull someone else up, you strengthen your own grip.

What Falling Down Looks Like

You will relapse—emotionally, mentally, maybe even physically. Here's what to do:

1. Acknowledge it. Don't justify. Don't dramatize.

2. Call your truth-teller within 24 hours.

3. Rest. Hydrate. Eat.

4. Ask, "What hole did I forget to fill?"

5. Update your plan.

Falling is inevitable. Staying down is optional.

The Numbers Don't Lie

- Recovery stabilization: ~5 years

- Median attempts: 2

- Relapse probability: 40-60%

- Time from first use to last use: ~27 years

Every step matters. Every attempt rewires the mind toward hope.

Healing from Abuse

Abuse teaches lies: *It was my fault. I'm alone. I'm unsafe.*

Recovery teaches truth: *It wasn't your fault. You're not alone. You can build safety.*

When you finally accept that your past pain isn't your fault but your healing is your responsibility, everything changes.

My Redemption Today

My life now is calm. My mornings are quiet. I lift weights, walk my dog, make coffee, and love my wife. I still fail, but I fall softer. My peace is simple, private, and earned daily.

At 27, I had a flashy life. At 52, I have a peaceful one. I'll take peace every time.

The Message

You are not your trauma. You are not your addiction. You are not your relapse. You are a man on the stairway—bruised, but climbing.

When no one else claps, tell your dog. He'll wag his tail like you won the Super Bowl.

Redemption isn't loud. It's sacred. Keep climbing.

Anthony James Hodel

Chapter 17:
Behind the Facemask

"Healing begins the day you stop performing for the world and start being honest with yourself."

The Real Reason I Wrote This Book

This book wasn't written for applause. It was written for release.

For most of my life, I lived like a man sprinting from a fire that only existed inside of me. I built businesses, chased perfection, and wore the image of success like armor. But the truth was simple — I was hurting, and I didn't know how to say it out loud.

Behind the Facemask isn't just my story — it's a mirror. It's for every man who wakes up tired of pretending, who's buried pain so deep that even success feels hollow. Every chapter before this — the childhood trauma, the addiction, the anger, the redemption — was a piece of the same puzzle. Each page was an excavation of truth. And this one… this is where the mask finally comes off.

A facemask protects you. It lets you stay in the game after the first hit, and maybe the tenth. But it also narrows your vision. It muffles your voice. It hides your eyes — the one place your truth can't play tough. I wore mine well. I learned how to outwork grief, outperform shame, and outtalk fear. I called it discipline. I called it standards. I called it leadership. Most days, it was just hiding.

The world rewards the mask. It loves clean numbers, closed deals, strong handshakes, and the man who *always* has it together. It doesn't see the cost—the distance at the dinner table, the apology that never gets said, the sleep you can't find, the faith you lost because you were too busy playing God in your own life. It doesn't see the boy inside the man, still waiting for someone to tell him he's allowed to be human.

I didn't write this book to be a guru. I wrote it because silence was killing me. Because I needed to name things that were naming me. Because pain grows in the dark, and the only way mine began to loosen its grip was by dragging it into the light and letting it be seen without excuses.

If you see yourself in any of this, hear me: you are not weak. You are not broken beyond repair. You're a man who learned to survive with the tools you had. The mask did its job. It kept you moving. It kept you safe. But at some point, the gear that kept you alive starts keeping you alone.

This is the chapter where I put mine down.

I'm not promising a fairy tale or a five-step formula. This isn't a hero's journey with a trumpet at the end. It's a man's journey — messy, repetitive, and often unglamorous. I still feel the itch to reach for the mask when the room gets quiet or the questions get close. The difference now? I notice it. I breathe. I tell the truth sooner. I pick people over image more often. And when I don't, I make amends instead of doubling down.

Here's what I *can* promise: I won't sell you a highlight reel. I'll show you the cut footage.

I will honor the mask for what it gave me, and I will refuse to let it define me.

- I will tell the truth when it makes me smaller, not just when it makes me look strong.

- I will choose connection over performance, even when performance pays better.
- I will ask for help before the house is on fire.

And here's the invitation I'm making to you — simple, not easy:

- Tell one person one true thing you've been avoiding.
- Name the thing you use to numb (work, workouts, whiskey, whatever) and don't reach for it for one hard hour.
- Make one amends you owe from your "armored" season. No speeches. Just responsibility.
- When your first instinct is to run, stay in the room for five more minutes.
- Find one man you trust and refuse to do this alone.

You don't have to write a book to take off the mask. Maybe yours looks like a conversation over coffee, a phone call you've dodged, a counseling appointment on a Tuesday, a letter you'll never send but needed to write. Maybe it looks like sitting with your son without a phone in your hand, or telling your wife you don't have an answer but you're willing to listen.

If a scoreboard matters here, it isn't followers, units sold, or standing ovations. It's a father who comes home with his whole face. It's a leader who tells the truth in rooms where truth is expensive. It's a man who stops outsourcing his worth to the next win and starts living like someone already loved. It's one generational pattern that ends because one man finally said, "Enough."

So this is the real reason I wrote *Behind the Facemask*: to stop living as a brand and start living as a man. To show you what it looks like — not because I've mastered it, but because I'm practicing it in public. If these pages do anything, I hope they give you permission to step into the light, to lay down what kept you safe, and to be seen as you are.

The mask served its purpose. Now let's see your face.

Why Men Must Speak

We were taught the wrong definition of strength. We were told real men don't cry. We were told to swallow pain like pride. We were told that admitting weakness meant losing respect. But silence kills. It eats at the inside of a man until he either explodes or disappears. I learned that the hard way.

For years, I turned pain into productivity — building, working, grinding. On the outside, it looked like ambition. But really, I was running from myself. Every goal became a hiding place. Every win was a way to distract from the loss inside. My mask looked like success, but behind it, I was suffocating.

We live in a world that confuses vulnerability with weakness. But real courage isn't lifting the most weight, earning the biggest check, or surviving without help. Real courage is telling the truth when every instinct tells you to shut up and smile. It's saying, "I'm not okay," and refusing to be ashamed of it. It's looking another man in the eye and letting him see that you bleed too.

Men don't need more silence. We need safety — spaces where honesty doesn't come with judgment, where tears aren't traded for ridicule, and where healing doesn't cost our dignity. We need conversations that start with truth, not ego. Because what we don't talk about will always own us.

Silence doesn't just hurt the man — it hurts everyone around him. Families break. Friendships fade. Sons learn that love looks stoic, and daughters grow up thinking men don't feel. When we don't speak, the damage echoes across generations. Pain unspoken becomes pain repeated.

When one man opens up, he gives permission for another to do the same. That's how generational silence ends — not with noise, but with truth. That's how healing begins — not in a therapist's office or a Sunday sermon alone, but in the quiet courage of men choosing honesty over image.

This isn't about weakness. It's about survival. It's about rewriting what it means to be a man — one conversation at a time. Because when men speak, we don't just save ourselves. We save the next generation from inheriting our silence.

So speak. Even if your voice shakes. Speak before the anger builds, before the bottle empties, before the mask cracks. Speak, because your story might be the key that unlocks someone else's prison. Speak, because strength isn't staying quiet — it's being brave enough to be heard.

When I Chose Calm

The day we took Sam to the vet for routine blood work, they brought him into the back and kept him there for a while. I looked at my wife and said, "What if he's back there dying?" Ten minutes later the vet walked in and said he'd coded. They had him on oxygen and believed he'd be okay, but told us to take him to the ER because they were understaffed. I was confused and numb.

We rushed Sam to the pet ER. His tongue was black. He was out of it. I drove through tears, hating myself for taking him in for a simple check-up. After six hours of waiting, the ER vet told us what had happened: the first clinic caused the crisis with the way they restrained him to draw blood, and they'd tubed him into his stomach. I spent $1,500 that day—$1,200 of it at the place that caused the problem.

I didn't respond in anger. I didn't care about the money. I just wanted Sam in my arms, coming home. I begged and prayed silently, and he came home—strong as ever.

A few days later it hit me: I didn't punch a wall. I didn't leave a scorched-earth review. I didn't call the credit card company. I wasn't handcuffed by anger anymore. I focused on the outcome. I believe in the universe and in the energy you put out. That day, I chose calm—and we brought our dog home.

Dopamine, the Next High — From Sex & Steroids to Service & Sweat

I used to think I had a self-control problem. What I really had was a chemistry problem. My nervous system had learned that dopamine—the brain's pursuit and motivation chemical—was the fastest road out of discomfort. Not joy. Not peace. Pursuit. That rising wave you feel before the drink, the hit, the hookup, the fight, the deal, the DM—that anticipation is dopamine. It's the wanting pathway, not the having one. And for years, my compass needle just spun toward whatever promised the biggest spike.

Sex as a Stimulus, not a Connection. I told myself I was wired different, that I just loved women. Truth? I loved the chase. Novelty drives dopamine—new faces, new danger, new secrecy. It wasn't intimacy; it was anesthesia. The moment after? Crash. Guilt. Shame. Then the loop: more seeking to outrun the comedown.

Steroids and the Mirage of Power. Exogenous testosterone can juice dopamine and blunt fear. You feel invincible—stronger, louder, less empathetic. That's not masculinity. That's chemistry with a steering wheel. The body pays, relationships pay, your future pays.

Anger as a Drug. People don't talk about this enough: rage is a high. It gives you a laser focus and an illusion of control. Your vision narrows, heart rate spikes, pain vanishes. For someone raised in chaos, that tunnel can feel like home. But anger's interest rate is brutal—legal fees, broken trust, shame, time you can't get back.

Here's the part I wish I'd learned in my twenties: dopamine is not the enemy. It's a survival signal. The problem isn't dopamine—it's what we've taught our bodies to chase when we feel empty, bored, anxious, or ashamed. If you don't design your highs, your history will do it for you.

What Works Now (The Sustainable Highs)

Movement as Medicine. Hard training gives me a cleaner, longer arc of dopamine—without the crash. Sprints, weights, long hikes, rucks. Add music, sunlight, or a partner and the neurochemistry compounds: endorphins (pain buffer), endocannabinoids (calm), and BDNF (brain fertilizer). Twenty minutes in, the fog lifts. Forty-five minutes in, my nervous system resets. The urge to self-destruct drops.

Cold, Breath, Sunlight. Short cold exposure often spikes dopamine and can stay elevated without the typical cliff. Box breathing or a long exhale pulls the nervous system out of the red. Morning light anchors circadian rhythm and mood.

Service and Skill. Helping someone else—teaching, mentoring, covering a bill, checking on a friend, volunteering—gives a steadier, warmer chemistry: dopamine with oxytocin (bonding) and serotonin (contentment). I call it the builder's buzz. It doesn't just make me feel better; it makes life better for someone else.

Create a Dopamine Menu. Two columns: Fast/Dirty (old hits—sex, rage, booze, chaos, gossip, gambling) and Clean/Stacked (training, cold + breath, real food, prayer or meditation, community work, creative work, nature, dog walks, reading, music, coaching). I don't pretend the first column isn't tempting. I design my day so the clean column is easier to reach, scheduled, and visible.

The 90-Second Rule. Cravings and surges crest and fall in about ninety seconds if you don't feed them with story. When the urge hits—name it, breathe for ninety seconds, move. If it's still there, call your person and say it out loud. Shame doesn't survive oxygen.

Replace, Don't Just Remove. Quitting a behavior without a substitute is like ripping out wires and expecting the lights to stay on. If you stop drinking, add walking. If you stop hooking up, add community and coaching. If you stop rage, add honest conversations and hard exercise. Biology hates empty space—fill it on purpose.

If I'd Known Then…

If I'd known that my willpower problem was a wiring pattern, I would've trained my nervous system, not just punished myself. I would've lifted earlier, slept more, told the truth sooner, and used service as a daily drug. Doing good isn't only moral—it's medicinal. I still love the high. I just stopped borrowing it. Today I earn it—through sweat, truth, and showing up for people who can't repay me. That's how I keep my chemistry honest and my soul intact.

What I Learned in College

College wasn't just an education in academics — it was an education in humanity. It was the first time I was far enough from the chaos to hear myself think. I started studying psychology out of curiosity, not knowing it would help me rebuild my own mind. In those classrooms, I learned about the human brain — how trauma embeds itself into the nervous system, how our reactions are often echoes of our past, how survival mode rewires our ability to trust.

I started connecting dots: why anger became my first language, why chaos felt safer than calm, why I feared peace — because I never knew it growing up. Understanding that trauma wasn't a choice — that it was conditioning — gave me compassion for myself. College didn't erase my pain, but it gave me words for it. And sometimes, having language for your suffering is the first step toward healing it.

Connecting the Past to Purpose

Every trauma carries potential energy — it can destroy you or drive you. For years, I let mine destroy me. Then I learned how to repurpose it. The pain that used to make me reckless now makes me disciplined. The anger that used to burn bridges now fuels passion. The guilt that used to haunt me now humbles me. When I turned that energy into building, mentoring, and serving others, I found what I had been chasing all along: purpose.

Every Day Is Still a Fight

Let's be real — healing isn't a straight line. It's a daily decision. There are still mornings when I wake up with old thoughts knocking on the door. Still nights when I replay conversations and wish I'd handled them differently. The difference now is awareness. I don't let emotions drive anymore — I let them ride shotgun. I acknowledge them, study them, then decide what happens next. Counseling taught me this rhythm — the power of the pause. It's not about suppressing emotion; it's about regulating it. That's emotional intelligence in action.

In the world behind the facemask, the battle isn't dramatic. It's ordinary. It's the email that sparks shame, the sideways comment that lights anger, the quiet afternoon that invites old habits. The mask wants back on every time control slips. My work now isn't to never feel that pull — it's to notice it sooner and choose differently, one small moment at a time.

The Rhythm I Practice

I keep it simple. Four steps I can remember when I'm tired:

1. **Notice** — "What am I feeling right now?" (Name it in a sentence, not a story.)
2. **Normalize** — "Of course I feel this; I'm human." (Permission reduces panic.)
3. **Navigate** — "What do I need?" (Water, walk, breath, break, truth.)
4. **Next Right Thing** — One choice that moves me toward integrity, not image.

That's it. Not a cure. A cadence.

The Power of the Pause

The pause is where I win or lose the day. It can be ten breaths, a sip of water, a slow walk to the end of the driveway — anything that interrupts autopilot.

- **Feel it without feeding it.** Emotions are data, not dictators.
- **Drop your shoulders.** Relaxed body, clearer brain.
- **Ask better questions.** "What story am I telling myself?" "What's the kindest truthful response available?"
- **Delay action.** I don't send "that" text. I draft it, breathe, and revisit when I'm steady.

Guardrails I Live By

I respect my limits because my limits keep me honest.

- **HALT check:** If I'm *Hungry, Angry, Lonely, or Tired*, I don't make big decisions.
- **No late-night truth-telling.** Nothing good starts with "I'll just say this real quick" after 10 p.m.
- **Move the body, move the mood.** A short walk beats another cup of coffee.
- **Repair fast.** If I blow it, I own it within 24 hours — no justifying, no "but you."
- **Ask for help early.** I text a trusted friend when the urge to isolate shows up.

When Old Patterns Knock

I still have triggers. They just don't get a key to the house anymore.

- **Work as numbing:** If I catch myself grinding to avoid feeling, I set a timer for ten minutes and sit with the emotion. Then I choose work with intention, not escape.
- **Anger as armor:** When I feel heat rise, I label it: *I'm angry because I feel dismissed.* Naming the wound redirects the weapon.
- **Shame as silence:** When shame says, "Hide," I do the opposite — I tell one true sentence to someone safe.

A Few Real-World Scenes

At home: I snap at my wife because I'm stressed. Old me would defend. New me pauses, breathes, and says, "I'm flooded. Give me ten minutes to reset." Then I come back and own it: "That tone was on me. I'm sorry." Repair beats being right.

At work: A deal falls through. The story in my head: *You're failing.* I write the story down, then challenge it: *What are the facts?* One lost deal doesn't equal a failed man. I make the next call.

Alone in the evening: Boredom invites old habits. I text a friend: "Not great tonight. Going for a walk." I swap scrolling for motion, pour water instead of whiskey, and put myself to bed on time. Boring choices save lives.

Regulating vs. Suppressing

Suppression pretends not to feel. Regulation tells the truth and chooses a response.

- **Suppressing** sounds like: *I'm fine. It's nothing.*

- **Regulating** sounds like: *I'm anxious and I'm going to slow down before I answer.*
  The difference is dignity. Suppression keeps the mask on. Regulation lets me be human and responsible at the same time.

Micro-Practices That Help

- **90-second reset:** Close eyes, breathe slow, feel feet on the floor. Let the surge pass.

- **Two-sentence journal:** "What happened?" "What did I need?" Done in under two minutes.

- **State the value:** "I choose connection over performance." Say it out loud; values direct behavior.

- **Ten-minute rule:** When an urge hits, wait ten minutes

before acting. Most waves pass if I don't feed them.

- **Gratitude, specific not grand:** Name three small gifts from today — not a speech, just a sentence each.

A Better Scoreboard

I don't measure perfection. I measure return time.

- How fast do I notice?
- How kind am I when I repair?
- How consistently do my actions match my values when no one's watching?
Shortening the distance between trigger and truth — that's progress.

What I Tell Myself on Hard Days

- *I don't have to win the day. I just have to choose the next right thing.*
- *Feel it fully; don't feed it foolishly.*
- *I can start over at any hour.*
- *The mask kept me safe. Honesty keeps me free.*

Questions for the Reader

If you're fighting too, here are prompts I use:

- What emotion shows up most often for you, and what need might it be pointing to?
- Where do you reach for the mask — at work, at home, with friends?
- What's one repair you could make this week without

explanation or defense?

- Who gets the text when you're not okay?

Healing for me isn't loud anymore. It's deliberate. It looks like drinking water before coffee, walking before arguing, apologizing before explaining, resting before unraveling. It looks like keeping my word to myself when no one's keeping score. Every day is still a fight — not against my feelings, but for my freedom. And the more I practice, the less I need the mask and the more I trust the man underneath it.

A Psychologist's Perspective

"You can't heal what you keep hidden, and you can't rewire what you keep reliving."

When I began trauma counseling, my therapist broke down my behavior in a way that rewired how I saw myself. She explained that my reactions weren't moral failures — they were neurological ones. Years of abuse had trained my brain to stay on high alert.

She told me, "Anthony, when you were young, your brain was programmed to protect you. It doesn't know you're safe now. That's why your body still reacts like you're in danger — even when you're not." That realization was liberating.

From a psychological standpoint, trauma imprints itself through implicit memory — stored not in words, but in sensations — the heart racing, the palms sweating, the instinct to fight or run. When a man experiences repeated abuse or betrayal, his body learns hypervigilance. He becomes reactive, not reflective. He confuses control with safety, dominance with confidence, and isolation with strength.

But psychology offers something powerful: reprogramming through awareness. Through Cognitive Behavioral Therapy (CBT) and Somatic Work, I learned how to slow my triggers. When my heart raced, I asked, what am I afraid of right now? When anger rose, I asked, is this about the present or the past? Over time, those questions became my emotional brakes.

My therapist also said, "Emotions are data, not directives. You don't have to act on them — just read them." That's when I stopped fighting myself and started understanding myself.

From a clinical perspective, the journey of a man healing from trauma involves three phases: Safety — Re-establishing control and predictability. Processing — Confronting the memories and the feelings. Reconnection — Rebuilding relationships and purpose. I've lived all three. And the final one — reconnection — is where I found peace.

Programming the Mind for Peace

Peace is not something you find — it's something you train for. I treat my mind like a muscle. Every morning, I feed it structure — reflection, prayer, gratitude, and stillness. I train my thoughts to stop sprinting toward chaos. Now, when stress hits, I don't break. I breathe. When anger whispers, I listen but don't obey. When fear shows up, I invite it to sit — but not stay. That's mental fitness.

The Power of Brotherhood

Men heal faster together. When one man speaks truth, another gains the courage to do the same. That's the power of brotherhood — shared struggle becomes shared strength. Brotherhood is medicine. We don't need to fix each other — just stand beside each other long enough to remind ourselves we were never alone.

Living Fulfilled — Even Alone

I used to confuse solitude with loneliness. Now I see it as strength. Silence isn't empty — it's where clarity lives. In those quiet hours, I learned that peace doesn't come from crowds, partners, or applause. It comes from alignment — when who you are inside finally matches who you show the world.

Self-Help Action Plan for Men Who Want to Heal

1. Accept What Happened — You can't outgrow what you won't face.

2. Seek Professional Help — Counselors are emotional trainers.

3. Find Accountability Brothers — Real men call out your excuses.

4. Build Structure — Routine builds peace.

5. Detach from Toxic People — Your peace is priority, not a privilege.

6. Forgive Yourself — You did what you had to do to survive.

7. Give Back — Service transforms scars into legacy.

Chapter 18:

Soul Under NDA

"Why My Spirituality Stays Confidential."

The Early Silence

I never talked much about God growing up. Not because I didn't know who He was — but because I didn't understand how He could let life happen the way it did.

As a kid, I saw things no child should ever see. I felt pain no one should ever feel. When you grow up surrounded by chaos, religion feels like a fairytale. It's hard to pray when you're living in what feels like hell already.

I used to think there was no devil — that this *was* hell on earth. The suffering, the violence, the confusion — it all felt like proof that heaven was a rumor told to keep people behaving.

My mom had her rosary, her candles, her prayer book. We went to church. I'd watch her whisper prayers while the smell of wax and incense hung in the air. But I saw through it at a young age. It looked like a performance. People dressed up for God on Sunday, then tore each other apart Monday through Saturday.

It didn't make sense to me. It didn't feel real.

Losing Faith Before Finding It

When you grow up in pain, you start to think God either forgot about you — or He was never there.

As a boy, I used to look at the cross and wonder: *If that man was the son of God, and He suffered like that, what chance do the rest of us have?*

I used to tell myself I didn't need saving. That maybe this was just the way things were. That good and evil lived in all of us, and faith was a game people played to make sense of their guilt.

But deep down, something in me was always reaching — like a hand pushing through darkness trying to grab onto something solid.

The Quiet Conversations

Even when I said I didn't believe, I talked to God. Not out loud, not in church, but in those quiet moments when everything hurt too much to carry.

I'd whisper things into the dark. "Give me strength." "Help me not be angry." "Help me make it through this one."

Over the years, that whisper became part of me — a silent ritual no one knew about. While I avoided religion, I never stopped seeking meaning.

I didn't need stained glass windows or priests to mediate it. I found God in the calm after a storm, in the sound of my own breath when I finally stopped fighting everything.

Why I Stayed Away from Church

I avoided churches because they reminded me too much of performance. People shouting "Amen" louder than they lived it. People who knew every verse but none of the meaning.

I've seen "Bible thumpers" hurt more people than the sinners they condemned. I've seen good people shamed for falling short by others who sin behind closed doors.

That kind of hypocrisy poisons faith. It turns something beautiful into theater. And I wanted no part of that.

Faith, for me, had to be personal. Real. Between me and Him. No noise, no audience, no collection plate. Just truth.

The Psychology of Faith and Healing

Psychologists talk about *meaning-making* — how humans find purpose after trauma. For many, that path leads back to spirituality, not necessarily organized religion.

When trauma strikes, it shatters the illusion of control. Faith — in any form — helps rebuild it. Studies show that prayer, meditation, or simply believing in something larger than oneself activates areas in the brain tied to calm and resilience.

I didn't know it then, but my quiet conversations with God were rewiring me. Each prayer — even the angry ones — gave my pain direction. Instead of festering, it started to heal.

There's power in surrender, especially when you've spent your life trying to control chaos.

The Wounds from Fake Religion

But fake religion can wound just as deep as abuse.

I've seen people use scripture like a weapon — twisting words meant for healing into instruments of judgment. That kind of faith doesn't lead people to God; it drives them away.

For years, I stayed away from anything that looked like that. The church gossip. The "holier-than-thou" posturing. The transactional faith that said, "If you give enough or say the right thing, God will love you more."

That's not love. That's marketing.

Real faith isn't a stage. It's a scar that still hurts but somehow reminds you that you're still alive.

The Return

It wasn't a pastor that brought me back to the Lord — it was quiet people. My grandmother. A few coaches. People who lived their faith instead of performing it.

They didn't lecture. They led by example. They showed me that being close to God doesn't mean being loud about Him.

When I finally started to listen, something shifted. I didn't see God as a punisher anymore. I saw Him as a quiet voice that had been there through every dark moment, whispering, *keep going*.

Every time I broke, He helped me rebuild. Not in lightning bolts or miracles — but in peace. That deep, still calm that hits you like sunlight after a storm.

The Calm After the Storm

Every time I talk to God now, that calm returns.

It's not dramatic. It's not cinematic. It's quiet — like a deep exhale after years of holding your breath.

And maybe that's what faith really is. Not certainty. Not perfection. But stillness — that feeling that, for one moment, you don't have to carry it all yourself.

The Power of Private Faith

I've never been one to broadcast my spirituality. It's not for show. It's for survival.

Every morning, I ask for strength, forgiveness, and a sharp mind to do good. And every day, I see His fingerprints on small miracles — a conversation that heals, a stranger helped, a problem solved just when I thought I was out of options.

This book? It's His answer to me.

For years, I heard that voice in the back of my head — "You have to do this." I ignored it. I doubted it. And finally, I obeyed it.

This chapter is my confession — not of sin, but of silence. Of keeping something sacred too long.

Faith and Psychological Renewal

Modern psychology now acknowledges what spiritual teachers have known for centuries: belief can heal.

- **Prayer** reduces stress hormones like cortisol and increases dopamine and serotonin — the same chemicals that regulate mood.

- **Faith communities** (when genuine) provide social support, reducing depression and anxiety.

- **Forgiveness** — a cornerstone of most religions — lowers blood pressure and improves heart health.

But here's the key: these benefits come from *authentic connection*, not ritual alone. When religion becomes performance, the brain doesn't heal — it hides.

So the work isn't about praying louder. It's about being honest — with yourself, with God, with your pain.

The False Prophets and Their Damage

Fake religion manipulates the vulnerable. It tells them their suffering is punishment, or that donations can buy redemption. It uses guilt as a leash.

That's not faith. That's fear dressed in a suit.

Real faith liberates. It forgives. It builds. It teaches you to love yourself even when you can't stand yourself.

If religion has ever hurt you, understand this: God didn't do that. People did. Don't confuse the two.

Action Plan: Quiet Faith in a Loud World

For readers walking their own path back to spirituality — here's what I've learned works:

1. Talk to Him privately.
You don't need a church pew to pray. You can do it while driving, walking, or washing dishes. Start with honesty, not perfection.

2. Practice daily gratitude.
List three things each day you're thankful for. Gratitude rewires the mind toward positivity.

3. Do one good deed daily.
Whether it's holding a door or helping someone in need, do good quietly. That's where faith breathes.

4. Avoid toxic faith spaces.
If a church or leader preaches fear, guilt, or superiority, walk away. Seek truth, not theatrics.

5. Reflect weekly.
Write a small journal entry or note — what went wrong, what went

right, and where you saw grace show up.

6. Forgive yourself often.
You can't hear God clearly when your mind is cluttered with shame. Forgiveness is the broom that clears the path.

7. Help without expecting applause.
Every selfless act draws you closer to the divine.

Coming Full Circle

I don't preach. I don't wear crosses. I don't post verses online. But every day, I live with faith.

My relationship with God doesn't need an audience. It needs authenticity.

I believe now that all the pain I endured wasn't proof of His absence — it was preparation for my purpose. This book is that purpose made real.

If you're reading this and you've ever wondered where God was during your worst moments, maybe this is your sign.

He was there — waiting for you to stop running, to start listening.

Because sometimes, faith doesn't shout. It whispers. And in that whisper, we find our peace.

Anthony James Hodel

Full Circle

When I started this journey, I thought success would heal me. It didn't. Truth did. Behind the facemask wasn't a monster — it was a man who finally forgave himself. That's what freedom looks like.

The Promise

I used to believe achievement could cauterize old wounds. Hit the number. Win the day. Add another line to the résumé. If pain is a leak, I thought, surely a wall of trophies will plug it.

The playbook was simple: outpace fear by outrunning it. I said yes to everything—flights that blurred together, meetings stacked so tightly they felt like Jenga, text messages answered at red lights and boarding gates. People called it drive. I wore the compliment like a medal and tried not to notice how heavy it felt around my neck.

Success did what success does. It bought distance—between me and the conversations I didn't want to have, between me and the mirror I avoided, between me and the boy I used to be. Distance can look like safety until you realize it's just another kind of loneliness.

What I wanted was healing. What I chased was applause. The applause was loud; the wound was quiet. It waited.

The Facemask

"Facemask" can mean a lot of things. Metal bars on a helmet. A tinted visor. A layer of cream that tightens and hides. Or the professional expression you slip on before walking into a room where the stakes are high and emotions are a liability.

My facemask was competence. Calm voice. Bullet-point answers. A suit tailored to say, *I belong here.* It kept me safe. It also kept me separate.

Masks aren't lies; they're strategies. They keep wind and debris out of your eyes so you can move through the world without flinching at every gust. The problem is when you forget to take them off. When you wear the same protection to the kitchen table that you wear to a negotiation. When the people who love you start talking to your strategy instead of to you.

For years, I confused being armored with being whole. I mistook control for courage. I believed that if I could predict every question, I'd never have to admit I didn't know an answer—especially the ones about myself.

The Bargain I Made

Underneath the hustle was a bargain I didn't know I'd signed: *If I become impressive enough, my history will stop chasing me.* Achievements would be my witness protection program. They would give me a new name and a new address. The past would lose the scent.

But bargains like that always come due. When the stage lights dim and the hotel door clicks shut, there's no crowd noise left to drown out the old narratives. You're left with the questions you've been too busy to ask:

- What am I protecting?

- Why am I so tired?

- When did "undeniable" become the only kind of love I trust?

I couldn't answer those with another win. I had to answer them with truth.

The Night the Noise Stopped

The turning point wasn't cinematic. There was no dramatic thunderclap. Just a quiet evening in a quiet room after a long day of being the person everyone expected. I set my phone facedown and watched the screen glow go dim like an ocean liner disappearing into fog.

There was a mirror across from the bed. I'd avoided it all week by turning off lights quickly and moving like a burglar in my own life. But that night I looked. Not a quick glance—an actual look. The mask did not shatter. The glass did not crack. The sky did not open. I just noticed that my eyes looked like they'd been holding their breath for years.

That was the truth I could handle. Not the whole truth. Just enough to start.

Telling the Truth (First to Myself)

Truth didn't arrive as a revelation; it arrived as a rhythm. Small, undramatic admissions I could say without running away.

- *I am excellent at performing calm and clumsy at feeling safe.*

- *I am generous with advice and stingy with vulnerability.*

- *I'm afraid if people saw the unpolished me, they'd walk away.*

The hardest part wasn't saying the words. It was sitting still after I said them. Not spinning them into meaning or drafting them into action plans. Just letting the truth be heavy on the table and not rushing to tidy it up.

I didn't become brave overnight. I became honest in increments. Courage, it turns out, is what grows in the space that honesty clears.

The Inventory

I've made a lot of lists in my life—goals, tasks, budgets, talking points. This one was different. I called it an "inventory" because that felt practical enough to trick me into doing it. I wrote down the moves I'd learned to survive:

- **Charm:** To be liked before I could be judged.

- **Competence:** To make myself useful so I couldn't be discarded.

- **Control:** To minimize surprises and keep panic at bay.

- **Speed:** To outrun reflection.

- **Silence:** To avoid saying what might not land well.

I didn't label these as sins. They were skills. They kept me alive. The problem was I used them everywhere—even in places I wanted to be known, not just safe. The inventory wasn't about condemnation; it was about precision. It helped me see where a skill had become a shield and where a shield had become a wall.

Then I made a second list—things I wanted to try instead:

- **Ask one more question** than usual when I feel defensive.

- **Say what I need** before resentment tells the story for me.

- **Choose "I don't know"** when I don't.

- **Let a silence sit** for three beats before I fill it.

Tiny practices, unglamorous and stubborn. This is what truth looks like when it goes to work.

The Conversations I Avoided

You can tell when a relationship has been talking to your mask. The conversations get efficient but thin. The jokes get safer. The calendar gets full of "later."

Truth changed that. Not all at once, not with everyone, but with enough people that my life started to feel less like a set and more like a room I lived in.

I began with a sentence I dreaded: "I need to tell you something I've been afraid to say." Then the simple version of the truth—no essay, no back-story to win a verdict. Sometimes there were tears. Sometimes there was relief. Sometimes there was a pause long enough for me to feel the urge to backpedal. I stayed.

I learned something crucial: amends are not apologies with extra adjectives. Amends are changed behavior over time. They are the unremarkable Tuesdays when you show up different.

Not everyone met me in that new place. Some liked the facemask better; it made everything predictable. That's okay. You can love people without wearing the armor they're comfortable with. You can keep your heart open without making it a revolving door.

The Younger Self at the Table

There is a boy in every man and a girl in every woman, waiting—sometimes politely, sometimes pounding—to be acknowledged. Mine lived at the edge of my choices, tugging at my sleeve, hoping I'd notice he was scared.

For a long time, I thought I had to outgrow him. Truth taught me something else: I had to include him.

One morning, before the inbox turned into a river, I made two cups of coffee—one for me, one for him—and sat as if he were across the table. I told him I was sorry for using him as fuel. I told him he didn't have to impress me anymore. I told him we were on the same team.

I expected the room to feel lighter. What I felt instead was steadier. As if a chair that had been missing a leg finally touched the floor.

Forgiving myself began there—not as a declaration, but as a posture. It sounded like *you're safe with me*. It felt like removing one piece of armor at a time and finding skin underneath that wasn't as fragile as I feared.

Work, Without the Costume

I worried that telling the truth would wreck my edge. Would honesty make me soft? Would forgiveness make me slow? Would taking off the mask mean I couldn't do the job?

Here's what happened instead. Meetings changed tone. I asked better questions because I wasn't busy proving I had answers. I started naming the tension everyone could feel but no one would say out loud. Teams exhaled.

Projects moved faster because we weren't wasting energy maintaining a fiction.

I stopped over-promising. I committed to fewer things and did them better. My calendar looked smaller and my days felt bigger. I no longer needed a win to justify a boundary. Boundaries weren't punishments anymore; they were accurate descriptions of what it would take to keep my word.

Clients—not all, but enough—noticed. They didn't hire me *in spite of* the truth; they hired me *because of* it. Authenticity isn't a brand. It's the relief people feel when there's nothing to decode.

The Body Remembers

Truth doesn't just change your mind; it changes your nervous system. For years, my body had been bracing. Jaw tight, shoulders high, breath shallow—like a runner waiting for a gunshot that might never come.

The earliest signs of healing were physical. I caught myself unclenching without giving the order. I slept like I used to when there were no deadlines, only summers that stretched. I noticed small, ordinary pleasures—steam rising from a mug, the way afternoon light crawls down a wall, the quiet labor of a ceiling fan. Freedom is often soluble in the smallest moments.

When old patterns flared, I learned not to shame them. Instead, I asked what they were trying to protect. Anxiety is a loyal guard dog; it just needs a new job description. I taught mine to sit by the door instead of pacing the hall.

Grief I Didn't Expect

Forgiveness didn't just bring relief; it brought grief. I had to say goodbye to versions of me that got me this far. The high-achiever who found safety in spreadsheets. The charmer who could turn any room friendly. The strategist who mistook contingency plans for intimacy.

Letting them retire felt like disloyalty at first. Then it felt like gratitude. You can't go full circle without honoring where you started. I thanked the roles for their service and told them they could rest. The room got quieter. The person left at the table was me.

The Practice of Gentleness

Gentleness used to sound like a soft skill. Now I think of it as precision. It's the ability to apply just enough force to match reality. Too much and you break what you mean to build. Too little and you never move anything that matters.

Practically, it looked like this:

- **Language audits.** I stopped calling mistakes "disasters" and started calling them "data."

- **Time audits.** I put fifteen unscheduled minutes between meetings so I wouldn't arrive everywhere already out of breath.

- **Attention audits.** I chose three priorities a day. Not seven. Not "as many as I can squeeze." Three.

Gentleness is not passivity. It's strength that isn't performing.

What Freedom Looks Like (Up Close)

Freedom didn't arrive as a single fireworks show. It showed up in mundane scenes that didn't make good television:

- Laughing mid-argument because I recognized an old pattern and said so.

- Telling a client, "I can't take that on and keep the quality you expect," and watching respect, not disappointment, land between us.

- Catching the reflex to make a point louder and choosing to listen instead.

- Walking past the mirror, unhurried, and not needing to look away.

Behind the facemask wasn't a monster. It was a human being who finally let himself be human. This is the paradox: the moment I stopped trying to be invulnerable, I became more trustworthy. People don't need perfection; they need presence.

A Field Guide for Coming Home

If I were to hand my earlier self a few notes for the road back, they would be simple:

1. **Name the mask.** Give it credit for what it protected. Then give it a hook by the door.

2. **Tell a small truth daily.** Not a performative confession. Just one honest sentence where you used to deflect.

3. **Practice endings.** Let a meeting end on time. Let a season end when it's over. Let a version of you end when it's done its job.

4. **Choose repair over performance.** Your best moments won't be flawless. They'll be the times you circle back and say, "I missed it—here's what I meant."

5. **Measure by aliveness.** If a win makes you smaller, it's not a win.

Circles, Not Ladders

I used to picture life as a ladder—up or down, higher or lower, worthy or irrelevant. The trouble with ladders is that you always look for the next rung. Even the view from the top feels like a preview for the next climb.

Now I think in circles: cycles of learning, seasons of expansion and rest, beginnings that look suspiciously like ends. To come full circle isn't to arrive where you started; it's to return with eyes that can finally see it.

The boy who needed the mask, the man who perfected it, the person who can hold it lightly—they're all me. The circle doesn't erase the earlier versions; it includes them.

The Choice I Keep Making

Truth isn't a finish line; it's a daily choice. Some mornings I reach for the mask by instinct. I remember how clean the edges felt, how clear the script was. Some days, I even put it on for a while. That's okay. The win is that I notice. I take it off sooner. I return.

Forgiveness, too, is not an event I can calendar and be done with. It's the posture I bring to my own history. It sounds like: *Of course you tried that. Of course it worked—for a while. Of course you want to protect yourself. And of course there's another way.*

The circle widens each time I choose that voice.

The Quiet Evidence

If you need metrics—and I often do—here are mine:

- **Fewer apologies for overcommitting.** Because I commit less and deliver more.

- **More laughter in rooms that used to be tense.** Because people trust what's plain.

- **Less reactivity.** Because I can feel without flailing.

- **More restful sleep.** Because the truth is not chasing me through the night.

Success still matters to me. I build, I ship, I lead. But success is no longer the surgeon. It's the side effect of a life aligned.

The Table, Set for Two

Sometimes I still pour two cups of coffee in the morning—the ritual that reminds me I'm not alone inside this one life. The younger me grins, less wary now. We plan the day like teammates. When the urge to perform flares, he nudges me and I smile. We're okay.

This isn't a fairy tale; it's a functional peace. It's the kind of freedom that lets you walk into a room without inventorying the exits. It's the kind of truth that steadies your hands when you reach for someone else's.

A Blessing for the Road

If I could hand you one line to carry when the noise gets loud and the mask feels necessary, it's this:

You are allowed to arrive unarmored.

Bring your skills; we'll need them. Bring your standards; they're good. But leave the bargain that told you, you had to be larger than life to be loved. The people who matter don't want the costume; they want you.

Full Circle

I started out thinking success would fix me. It didn't. Truth did. Not a sterile, courtroom truth designed to win a case, but the kind of truth that lets you breathe.

Behind the facemask wasn't a monster. It was a person waiting to be forgiven by the one judge who mattered—himself. The circle closed not with a cheer but with a quiet yes: *I will live from who I am, not from who I'm performing to be.*

That's what freedom looks like.

Letter to My Brothers

"You're not alone in the silence anymore."

To every man who reads this: I see you. I've been you. And I believe in who you're becoming. You don't owe the world your perfection. You owe yourself your peace.

This is a letter of invitation, not indictment; a field guide, not a rulebook. You will not find perfectionism here. You will find language for the things you've felt but haven't said, and practical steps to build friendships, repair relationships, and reclaim inner peace.

If you're in immediate crisis or thinking about harming yourself: please seek help now from local emergency services or a trusted professional in your area. Your life matters. You matter.

The Silence We Inherited

Most men learned early to hold their breath around pain. We were taught to tighten the jaw, square the shoulders, and swallow the words that threatened to tremble out. The silence was sold to us as strength. Sometimes it even worked—until it didn't. The quiet that once hid our fear began to hide our hearts. We got good at disappearing, even while standing right there.

Silence isn't just the absence of sound; it's the absence of witness. Without a witness, our stories harden into private burdens. We misread our pain as proof that we're failing at being men, when in truth it's proof that we are human.

This letter is a doorframe. If you've been pacing the room of your life without a way out, consider this your threshold. Step over it with whatever you're carrying. The only password is honesty.

Practice & Prompts

- Write down one thing you're tired of hiding.

- Text someone you trust: "Can we talk this week? I want to share something real."

- Stand in front of a mirror and say, "I'm allowed to be seen."

Perfection vs. Peace

Perfection is a moving target that keeps you sprinting until you forget why you started. Peace is the ability to stop running without losing yourself. Perfection trades intimacy for image; peace trades image for integrity. Perfection is brittle. Peace bends and breathes.

You don't owe the world a spotless story. You owe yourself the practice of becoming whole. That practice includes mistakes, apologies, course corrections, and grace. When you prioritize peace, you choose the long road of alignment over the short sprint of approval.

Practice & Prompts

- Finish this sentence: "If I stopped chasing perfection, I would…"

- Identify one recurring situation where you perform instead of connect. Plan a different response.

- Replace "I should" with "I choose" for a day. Notice the shift.

Naming What Hurts

A man with words for his inner world is harder to drown. Many of us weren't given the vocabulary for our feelings, so every emotion became "stress," "anger," or "I'm fine." Naming helps us right-size what's happening: "I'm disappointed," "I'm ashamed," "I'm lonely," "I'm scared." With names, the fog becomes a map.

Language doesn't make you soft; it makes you precise. Precision opens choices. When you can say, "I'm anxious because I don't know what's coming," you can ask for clarity. When you can say, "I'm hurt because I felt dismissed," you can ask to be heard. The goal isn't to wallow—it's to orient.

Practice & Prompts

- Write a two-column list: Left = Common triggers. Right = Emotions. Draw lines connecting them.

- Keep a small "word bank" on your phone: frustrated, overwhelmed, ashamed, lonely, afraid, hopeful. Use it daily.

- Share one specific feeling with a friend this week.

The Myth of "I've Got This"

Hyper-independence looks like strength until it looks like isolation. "I've got this" is helpful in a crisis; it's harmful as a lifestyle. Men who try to carry everything alone eventually drop something that matters—health, marriage, friendship, self-respect.

Asking for help is not outsourcing your manhood; it's treating your life as a team sport. The best leaders recruit support. The best athletes rely on coaches and spotters. The best brothers learn to receive as readily as they give.

Practice & Prompts

- Identify one load you can share this week—childcare, finances, a home repair, a difficult call.

- Write three names of people who could be part of your "board of advisors." Reach out to one.

- Practice this sentence: "I can lead this, but I can't do it alone."

Friendship as a Practice

Male friendships often stall at banter and logistics. We need richer soil. Depth requires intention: recurring time, agreed rules, and shared vulnerability. A good friend won't save you from every storm, but he will save you from facing storms alone.

Friendship is built in the mundane. Show up. Remember details. Follow up on the hard thing he shared last month. Tell the truth with care. Celebrate without envy. Mourn without advice.

Practice & Prompts

- Put a monthly "brother breakfast" on the calendar. Non-negotiable.

- Try "rose, thorn, bud" (win, challenge, hope) at your next meet-up.

- Choose one friend and ask, "What's one way I can support you this month?"

Love Without Keeping Score

Scorekeeping kills intimacy. When love becomes accounting—who did more, who owes what—we drift from partnership into rivalry. Real love collaborates. It counts the cost together and shares the credit.

To love without keeping score, we need boundaries (what I can give) and visibility (what we both need). When we share limits and desires openly, we build trust. When we assume and hoard resentment, we build walls.

Practice & Prompts

- With your partner or closest friend: "Here's what I'm capable of this week; here's what I'm not."

- Ask: "What would make you feel most supported right now?"

- Replace "You never…" with "When X happens, I feel Y, and I need Z."

Anger, Power, and Gentleness

Anger is a signal, not a strategy. It can point to violated values, hidden grief, or untreated fear. Unowned anger leaks as sarcasm, withdrawal, or explosions. Owned anger becomes boundary, clarity, and courage.

Gentleness is not weakness—it is power under control. It allows us to be strong without being sharp. We can be firm about what matters and soft on the people we love.

Practice & Prompts

- Notice the first signs of anger in your body (heat, tight jaw, tunnel vision). That's your early alert.

- Develop a short reset ritual: step away, drink water, breathe for 60 seconds.

- After anger, repair: "I'm sorry for how I spoke. Here's what I was feeling and what I'll do next time."

Work, Worth, and "Enough"

Work is noble. Worshiping work is destructive. When our worth rides on performance, we grind until our gears strip. The question is not, "How do I do more?" but "What is enough, right now, for a life I respect?"

Enough is a boundary against the endless appetite of achievement. Without it, we never arrive. With it, we can work hard during work and be fully present at home. We trade constant hustle for focused seasons.

Practice & Prompts

- Define "enough" for this quarter: income, hours, weekends off.

- Choose one "closing ritual" at day's end: a walk, a summary note, shutting the laptop and touching a doorknob.

- Ask weekly: "What mattered most, and did I give it time?"

Fathers, Sons, and Repair

Our fathers gave us gifts and gaps. Some of us received tenderness and teaching; some learned survival. Either way, we carry those patterns forward—until we choose to repair. Repair doesn't rewrite the past; it reroutes the future.

Becoming a better man than your history predicted is a quiet revolution. It starts with honesty, continues with boundaries, and matures into forgiveness (sometimes from a distance). If you are a father, let your children see you apologize. Let them watch you regulate, rest, and recommit.

Practice & Prompts

- Write a two-part letter (you don't have to send it): "What I received; what I needed."

- Name one generational pattern you will end. Choose one practice that replaces it.

- If it's safe, tell your father or a father figure one thing you appreciate and one boundary you need.

Grief and Letting Go

Grief is the tax love pays for having mattered. Men often try to outwork grief or drown it in distractions. But grief waits. When we feel it on purpose, it moves. When we avoid it, it multiplies.

Tears are not surrender—they are release. Rituals help: lighting a candle, speaking a name, creating a memorial playlist, writing a goodbye letter. Letting go is not betrayal; it's honoring what was by making room for what will be.

Practice & Prompts

- Name what you've lost (person, season, identity). Say it out loud.

- Create a small ritual of remembrance this month.

- Share your grief with one trusted person and ask them simply to listen.

A North Star: Values You Can Stand On

When you don't know your values, you borrow someone else's urgency. Values are the rails your life runs on. They don't remove difficulty; they remove confusion. When choices pinch, values decide.

Pick a handful you can actually live: integrity, curiosity, service, courage, presence. Define them in your own words. Then let your calendar, not your captions, reveal what you value most.

Practice & Prompts

- Choose five values. For each, write a sentence that starts, "I live this value when I…"

- Audit last week's calendar against your values. What aligns? What needs pruning?

- Share your top three values with a friend. Ask for accountability.

Your Body Keeps the Score (Sleep, Food, Stress)

You can't outthink a nervous system that's on fire. Sleep is emotional first aid. Movement wrings anxiety from the body. Food is information. Hydration is mood regulation. These are not lifestyle hacks; they're the ground floor.

Treat your body like a teammate, not a tool. Instead of punishing it for underperforming, ask what it needs to perform. Often the answer is humble: earlier bedtime, sunlight, a walk after meals, real conversations, fewer screens at night.

Practice & Prompts

- This week: 10 minutes of morning light, a brisk daily walk, a consistent sleep window.

- Keep a "stress reset" list: breathwork, pushups, stretching, prayer or quiet.

- Before a hard conversation, eat, hydrate, and move for five minutes.

Courageous Conversations (Scripts)

Silence cracks when we speak with care. Here are templates you can borrow and make your own.

To a friend (opening up):
"Can I share something real? I've been carrying _____. I don't need you to fix it, just hear me out. If you have questions after, I'm open."

To a partner (repair):
"When _____ happened, I felt _____ because _____. I'm sorry for _____. What I want is _____. What would help us move forward?"

To a boss (boundary):
"I want to deliver great work and sustain it. To do that, I need _____. Here's a plan I propose: _____. Can we align on this?"

To yourself (reframe):
"I can handle this one step at a time. I can ask for help. I can rest without quitting."

Practice & Prompts

- Choose one conversation you've avoided. Write the first sentence.

- Schedule it. Prepare with a walk and a clear ask.

- Debrief afterward: What did I learn? What will I try next time?

Boundaries and Standards

Boundaries protect what you value; standards express who you are. A boundary says, "This is what I can and cannot do." A standard says, "This is how I do it." Without boundaries, resentment grows. Without standards, self-respect shrinks.

Boundaries are best delivered early, clearly, and kindly. Standards are best maintained consistently and quietly. Both are forms of self-leadership.

Practice & Prompts

- Write one personal boundary for time, one for tech, one for money.

- Define three standards you'll uphold even when no one is watching.

- Practice saying, "That doesn't work for me. Here's what does."

Building Circles of Brotherhood

A circle is stronger than a crowd. Crowds cheer you; circles carry you. A brotherhood has three ingredients: rhythm (we meet regularly), rules (we keep confidentiality; we tell the truth), and roles (we take turns leading, listening, and challenging).

Start small: three to five men, 60–90 minutes monthly. Use a simple frame—check-in (feelings), topic (one man's real life), commitment (one action each), closing (gratitude). Over time, trust compounds.

Practice & Prompts

- Invite two men for a trial month.

- Agree on rules: confidentiality, no fixing without permission, equal airtime.

- Decide a cadence and stick to it.

When the Floor Drops Out (A Crisis Plan)

Crisis is not the time to invent a plan. Build one now. Keep it simple and visible.

Personal Signals: Can't sleep for days, recurring thoughts of harm, substance spiral, panic that won't subside.
Immediate Steps:

1. Remove yourself from harm (leave the room/house, pause the car).

2. Call a trusted person from your list.

3. If danger feels immediate, contact local emergency services or go to the nearest emergency department.
   Aftercare: Tell one more person. Book an appointment with a qualified professional. Rest, hydrate, and simplify for 72 hours.

Practice & Prompts

- Create a "three names" list in your phone.

- Write your top three early-warning signs. Share them with your circle.

- Decide now where you would go in an emergency.

A Blueprint for Peace (Daily/Weekly Practices)

Peace is built by rhythm, not heroics. Here's a simple blueprint you can adapt.

Daily (30–45 minutes total):

- **Morning:** 10 minutes light/movement; name your top 3 values for the day.

- **Midday:** 3-minute reset (breathing, water, brief stretch).

- **Evening:** 5-minute review—What mattered? What needs repair tomorrow?

Weekly:

- One hour of deep friendship time.

- One hour of planning (money, meals, schedule).

- One hour of play or learning that has nothing to do with your job.

Monthly:

- A half-day personal retreat: reflect, reset, recommit.

- A check-in with your "board of advisors."

Practice & Prompts

- Put these blocks in your calendar as recurring events.

- Track your "peace meter" (0–10) each night; note what raised or lowered it.

- Share your blueprint with someone who will nudge you when you drift.

Closing Letter

Brother/Sister,

If you've read this far, you've already done something brave. You've turned toward your life with your eyes open. That matters.

You don't need to become a different man to be worthy of love, rest, or joy. You are already worthy. Growth isn't an audition; it's stewardship. It's caring for what you've been given—your body, your voice, your relationships, your work—so that you can offer the world something true.

Remember: you're not alone in the silence anymore. Experiment with the practices in these pages. Adjust, adapt, and keep going. When you fall short, repair. When you succeed, celebrate. When you're unsure, ask. When you're tired, rest. And when you doubt, borrow my belief for a while: you are capable of good, strong, gentle things.

s

With strength, love, and solidarity,
— **Anthony James Hodel**

The 44 Foundation Legacy Pledge

"We heal by helping others heal."

The 44 Foundation was born from the same fire that forged this story — from the ashes of pain, the lessons of redemption, and the unwavering belief that healing becomes real only when it's shared. *Behind the Facemask* is not just a book — it's a movement, a blueprint, and a call to action for every man who has ever carried unspoken pain behind strength's disguise.

The 44 Foundation exists for those men, for the youth who will become them, and for the families and communities who stand beside them. Its mission is simple, but powerful: **to turn pain into purpose, and silence into support.**

Our Purpose

We live in a world where men are taught to suffer quietly — to hold it together, to "man up," to never show the cracks. But those cracks are where the light gets in. The 44 Foundation was created to catch that light and redirect it — to guide men out of the shadows of shame and into the freedom of truth, healing, and hope.

The number **44** represents transformation — a bridge between what was broken and what can be rebuilt. It stands for second chances, for strength through vulnerability, and for the kind of legacy that isn't written in wealth or accolades, but in lives changed.

Our Mission

The mission of The 44 Foundation is to provide:

- **Emotional Support Programs** for men and young boys struggling with trauma, addiction, anger, or loss.

- **Scholarships & Sponsorships** for mental health counseling, therapy, and mentorship opportunities.

- **Community Outreach** initiatives to build safe spaces for dialogue — in schools, barbershops, churches, and locker rooms.

- **Education & Awareness** through workshops and media partnerships that teach emotional intelligence, accountability, and the art of healthy masculinity.

- **Rehabilitation Partnerships** with treatment centers and organizations that help men rebuild their lives after incarceration, substance abuse, or domestic instability.

Our Promise

Every man deserves a place to speak without fear, to heal without judgment, and to be reminded that redemption isn't a miracle — it's a daily decision.
When you join The 44 Foundation, you're not just donating to a cause — you're becoming part of a **movement of men helping men**. You're standing up to say:

"I've worn the mask. I've carried the weight. Now I choose to help others set theirs down."

We pledge to invest every resource — time, money, and heart — into real impact:

- One man lifted.

- One youth guided.

- One generation changed.

The Legacy We're Building

The 44 Foundation is committed to breaking generational cycles — of silence, of shame, of self-destruction. Through programs, mentorships, and storytelling, we're building a community where men can evolve into leaders, fathers, brothers, and friends who heal instead of hide.

We believe the next generation shouldn't have to unlearn the same lessons we did. They deserve to see that real strength is found in accountability, kindness, and courage — not in pretending everything's fine. Our legacy will not be measured by the number of followers or fundraisers, but by the number of lives rebuilt because we dared to start the conversation.

How You Can Help

If *Behind the Facemask* spoke to you — if you saw yourself in these pages — then this is your invitation to do something with that recognition.

You can pledge your support at:

www.behindthefacemaskbook.com

Final Words

You can't rewrite your past. But you can redirect your future.

You can't change where you came from. But you can change what grows from it.

You can't erase the scars. But you can show the world how you healed.

And maybe — just maybe — someone watching you rise will finally believe they can too.

Anthony James Hodel

Afterword

Writing this book was like ripping open wounds that I spent decades trying to bury under anger, addictions, and distractions. Each chapter forced me to sit with memories I once tried to drink away, fight away, or cover up with muscle, money, or women. To write these pages, I had to relive the footsteps in the hallway, the slammed doors, the shame, the rage, and the bad decisions that followed me like shadows.

But I also had to relive the lifelines—the ride to football practice that saved me, the coaches who saw something worth investing in, the grandmother who gave me refuge, the wife who gave me another chance, and the rare moments when God's hand was so obvious it could not be denied.

This book isn't just about me. It's about anyone who has ever felt trapped by their past, betrayed by people who were supposed to protect them, or poisoned by shame so heavy it steals their breath. If you saw yourself in these pages, know this: your story isn't over.

One of the hardest lessons I learned is that healing isn't a destination—it's a daily decision. Redemption doesn't come in one grand gesture. It comes in the small moments: choosing honesty over silence, choosing sobriety over the bottle, choosing forgiveness over rage, choosing to break cycles instead of repeating them.

When I look back, I don't see a perfect man. I see a broken boy who clawed his way through life, often in the wrong direction, until grace found him. I see someone who failed, hurt others, and burned bridges—but also someone who kept walking, who finally stopped running from himself, and who decided to turn pain into purpose.

If there's one message I want this book to leave behind, it's this: no matter where you start, no matter how ugly your story has been, you can rewrite the ending. You can turn trauma into testimony, failures into fuel, and shame into strength.

I wrote Behind the Facemask not to glorify the scars, but to show that scars prove survival. They prove that the abuse didn't win, the addictions didn't define me, and the shame didn't silence me forever.

My hope is that when you close this book, you don't just see my redemption stairway—you see the first step of your own.

—Anthony James Hodel

About the Author

Anthony James Hodel is a former college and professional arena football player turned award-winning entrepreneur, consultant, and philanthropist. Born and raised in Cleveland, Ohio, he overcame an abusive childhood and life-altering struggles to build a legacy of resilience, redemption, and leadership.

As CEO of Hodel Holdings, LLC, Anthony has guided multiple ventures across the automotive, finance, and sports sectors. He is also the founder of the Athletic Scholarship Corporation (ASC), an international sports marketing agency dedicated to helping student-athletes earn college opportunities.

Anthony's career includes recognition as Ernst & Young Entrepreneur of the Year, Weatherhead 100 1 Company, Wall Street Journal Businessman of the Year (2002–2004), and features on national media outlets including the Winner's Circle with Terry Bradshaw.

Beyond business, Anthony is a passionate mentor. He has worked with countless athletes, coaches, and families nationwide—turning his personal pain into a platform to inspire and empower others. His memoir, Behind the Facemask: A Child's Abuse, A Man's Redemption, blends raw storytelling with life lessons, offering readers both a window into survival and a roadmap to healing.

Anthony lives with his wife, Trisha, and continues to balance his love for business, travel, sports, and giving back through his philanthropic work with The 44 Foundation and other charitable organizations.

Follow Anthony online: www.behindthefacemaskbook.com

Anthony James Hodel

Index

A

Abuse, 1–2, 5, 11, 19, 21, 23, 25, 27, 31, 33, 35, 37, 39, 41, 43, 45, 47, 51, 53, 55, 59, 61, 63, 65, 67, 69, 71, 75, 77, 79, 81, 85, 87, 89, 91, 94–95, 97, 99, 101, 103, 105, 109–111, 113, 115, 117, 119, 123, 125, 127, 129, 131, 133, 135, 137, 139, 141, 143, 147, 149, 151, 153, 155, 157, 159, 161, 163, 165, 169, 171, 173, 175, 177, 179, 183, 185, 187, 189, 193, 195, 197, 199, 203, 205, 207, 211, 213, 215, 217, 219, 221, 223, 225, 227, 229, 233, 235, 237, 239, 241, 243, 245, 249, 251, 253, 255, 257, 259, 261, 263, 265, 267, 269, 271, 273, 275, 277, 279, 281, 283, 293

Anger, 7, 36, 61, 68, 70, 109, 116, 128, 152, 163, 172, 176, 191, 194, 197–198, 239, 245, 270–271

Anna Nicole Smith, 77

B

Body Remembers, 260

Broken Boys, 73

Business, 144, 150

C

Chief Marketing Officer, 9

Child, 7, 22, 68, 192, 209

Church, 57, 247, 252

Cleveland, 1–2

Coach, 48, 66, 159

Coach McPhie, 66

Control, 78, 80, 86, 141, 155, 192, 236

Court, 121, 155, 212

D

Dr Dwyer, 89–90

E

Entrepreneur, 15, 289

F

Facemask, 1–2, 5, 11, 19, 21, 23, 25, 27, 31, 33, 35, 37, 39, 41, 43, 45, 47, 51, 53, 55, 59,

61, 63, 65, 67, 69, 71, 75, 77, 79, 81, 85, 87, 89, 91, 95, 97, 99, 101, 103, 105, 109, 111, 113, 115, 117, 119, 123, 125, 127, 129, 131, 133, 135, 137, 139, 141, 143, 147, 149, 151, 153, 155, 157, 159, 161, 163, 165, 169, 171, 173, 175, 177, 179, 183, 185, 187, 189, 193, 195, 197, 199, 203, 205, 207, 211, 213, 215, 217, 219, 221, 223, 225, 227, 229, 233, 235, 237, 239, 241, 243, 245, 249, 251, 253, 255, 257, 259, 261, 263, 265, 267, 269, 271, 273, 275, 277, 279, 281, 283, 293

Faith, 104, 172, 250, 252

Family, 70, 73, 76, 102, 171, 193, 204, 207, 212

Father, 4, 7, 15, 18–19, 42, 101–102, 121, 171–173, 196, 209–210, 212–213, 215, 233, 272

Fear, 18, 31, 34, 68, 77, 81, 89, 111, 130, 159, 201, 231, 252, 282

Finance, 9, 146

Finance Manager, 9

Football, 4, 13, 42, 54–55, 59, 63–64, 68, 70, 150, 214

Forgiveness, 23, 272

G

Grandpa Ray, 136–138

Guilt, 10, 19, 64, 128, 157, 176, 248, 252

H

Healing, 58, 90, 100, 112, 158, 163, 170, 172, 205, 227, 239, 245, 254, 260, 281, 287, 292

Home, 3, 15, 17–18, 22, 24, 29–30, 32, 37, 39, 42–43, 48–49, 51–52, 54, 57–58, 60, 64, 66, 68, 73, 84, 86, 102, 111, 123, 145, 147, 152, 156, 159, 170, 173, 186, 193, 197, 199, 209–210, 213–214, 222, 224–225, 236–237, 243, 269, 271, 291

Hope, 15–16, 45, 96, 123, 229, 233, 269, 281, 288, 292

I

Injury, 22, 35–36

J

James Hodel, 289

Johnny Knox, 73

L

Lake Erie League, 52

Legacy, 101, 162, 202, 205, 207, 246, 281, 283

Lies, 29, 57, 107, 117, 171, 182, 255

M

Marketing, 9, 151

Mask, 43, 224

Meeting Big Mike, 76

Mexico, 7, 15, 168

Mother, 18, 22, 49

O

Ohio, 1–2, 168

P

Police, 30, 85, 225

Purpose, 53, 145, 158, 161–162

R

Redemption, 1, 5, 11, 19, 21, 23, 25, 27, 31, 33, 35, 37, 39, 41, 43, 45, 47, 51, 53, 55, 57, 59, 61, 63, 65, 67, 69, 71, 75, 77, 79, 81, 85, 87, 89, 91, 95, 97, 99, 101, 103, 105, 109, 111, 113, 115, 117, 119, 123–125, 127, 129, 131, 133, 135, 137, 139, 141, 143–144, 147, 149, 151, 153, 155, 157, 159, 161, 163, 165, 169, 171, 173, 175, 177, 179, 183, 185, 187, 189, 193, 195, 197, 199, 203, 205, 207, 211, 213, 215, 217, 219, 221, 223–227, 229, 233, 235, 237, 239, 241, 243, 245, 249, 251, 253, 255, 257, 259, 261, 263, 265, 267, 269, 271, 273, 275, 277, 279, 281, 283, 293

S

Scared Straight, 40

School, 213

Shame, 7, 16, 103, 118, 127, 237, 241

St Ignatius, 51

St Jude's, 203–204

T

Team, 41, 51, 59, 68, 96, 107, 147, 158–159, 199, 259

Therapy, 16, 27, 33, 35, 47, 100, 114, 145, 151, 193–194, 206, 223

Trauma, 25, 33, 47, 54, 68, 88, 93–94, 96, 100–104, 113–114, 117–119, 125–126, 175, 194, 201, 239, 245, 249

Truth, 3, 10, 18–19, 21, 23, 27, 38, 43, 45, 57, 62, 65, 83–86, 90, 93, 97–99, 102, 104, 107, 109, 113, 115, 117, 119, 123, 126–127, 151, 162, 170–171, 179, 182, 184–186, 193–194, 196, 204, 210, 214, 226–229, 231–235, 238, 242–243, 245, 249, 256–260, 262, 264–266, 269, 276, 281, 293

U

United States, 2

V

Vince Lombardi, 62

W

Warrior Project, 203

Woman, 19, 193, 259

Work, 2, 17, 21, 23, 25, 84–85, 117, 141, 155, 196, 198, 201, 223, 243, 259, 271, 276

Y

Young Entrepreneur, 289

Z

Zip Code Sam, 75

PERSONAL NOTES

Anthony James Hodel

PERSONAL NOTES

PERSONAL NOTES

Anthony James Hodel

PERSONAL NOTES

www.ingramcontent.com/pod-product-compliance
Lightning Source LLC
Chambersburg PA
CBHW050523100526
44581CB00002B/87